D1055367

Adult Education

THE LIBRARY OF EDUCATION

A Project of The Center for Applied Research in Education, Inc.

Categories of Coverage

I	II	III
Curriculum and Teaching	Administration, Organization, and Finance	Psychology for Educators
IV	V	VI
History, Philosophy, and Social Foundations	Professional Skills	Educational Institutions

Adult Education

COOLIE VERNER

Professor of Adult Education
University of British Columbia

with the assistance of

Alan Booth

Research Associate
Adult Education Research
The University of Nebraska

The Center for Applied Research in Education, Inc.
New York

Fifth Printing.....April, 1969

Library of Congress
Catalog Card No.: 64-11025

PRINTED IN THE UNITED STATES OF AMERICA

Foreword

Just as everybody is against sin, so nowadays is everybody for adult education. Just as the forces arrayed against sin are often divided, confused, and ineffectual, so the support for adult education, though quite general, is divided, confused, and ineffectual. Yet the belief in the value of continued learning by adults has been with us in the Western world in one way or another for at least two centuries. Groups who have recognized these needs have moved in various way to meet them, whether in the Mechanics Institutes of Britain, the far earlier efforts of artisans in a few western Massachusetts communities, the more recent agricultural and home economics extension services, or in a myriad of other institutions or agencies. But, as Professor Verner shows, both the very multiplicity of these agencies and the uncertainty of their permanence have handicapped the development of a strong and coordinated system of adult education in the United States.

Nor should this situation, though regrettable, occasion surprise. It took decades for our society to decide that age-old education by mothers' precepts and imitation of fathers' work should be supplemented for all by the three *R*'s taught in a school at public expense. Even this step was not accepted with alacrity by all the states. It took about one hundred and fifty years for the last of the original thirteen colonies to make elementary education a responsibility of society. Nor was Horace Mann's eloquent advocacy of what we now know as high schools immediately convincing to the self-reliant settlers of this continent. Mort, taking nine now accepted newer elements in the curricula of our schools, showed that in Pennsylvania, from the time the first school system adopted one of these subjects until more than half taught it, an average of half a century elapsed.[1]

No social institution is closer to the society that created it than

[1] Paul R. Mort and Francis G. Cornell, *American Schools in Transition* (New York: Teachers College, Bureau of Publications, Columbia University, 1941).

is education. Every member of the society has had a definite experience in school. All parents experience it again through their children. Many are vocal about what it should do and be. Its schools, more than any other social institution, reflects what the community is. Like elementary and high school education, adult education will become firmly rooted in American society when enough people seeking to understand the problems of a tortured world, or trying to keep abreast of accelerating social and technological change, or simply eager to remedy deficiencies in their own education, demand it. In a society that has achieved the measure of democracy ours has, adult education can win its destined place in the educational sun in no other way. But its leaders can stimulate and accelerate the process if they are well grounded in the behavioral sciences.

Professor Verner makes the social and community foundations of adult education quite clear and unmistakable in his succinct, streamlined discussion. The handicaps and problems of adult education and the errors of adult educators are not minimized but faced as, unfortunately, too few adult educators have yet had the courage and the wisdom to do. Methods and techniques are differentiated, and the general fuzziness in this area of operations is clarified by precisely defined conceptualization. The strategic ways for adult education to advance are pointed out with confidence in the eventual success of the movement, inchoate as it is today. Throughout, the generalizations offered are based on findings of research bearing on or concerned with adult education in a number of disciplines. Thus wishful thinking, a besetting sin of too many in adult education, is exorcised. The field should profit greatly from this work.

EDMUND deS. BRUNNER

Adult Education

Coolie Verner

This volume on adult education gives broad coverage of an important aspect of American education. Along with other volumes on elementary education, secondary education, and higher education in the Library of Education series, all levels of education are included.

The book begins with a discussion of the scope, need, functions, and institutions that provide adult education. It follows with an analysis of the adult learner and the adult education teacher. Another section of the book deals with the kinds of learning especially appropriate for adults, the methods and teaching techniques which are appropriate, and the administration and supervision of such programs.

The author, Coolie Verner, and Alan Booth who assisted with the writing, have prepared an authoritative and interesting book. It is an up-to-date and ready source of information, experience, and practice in adult education. The book will be useful to teachers, school administrators, community leaders, and all adults interested in continuing education.

The two final chapters on evaluation and problems and prospects anticipate the improvement of adult education programs. This book is unique in that it looks to the future when adult education "will become such an integral part of human existence that all mankind will be learning systematically all the time."

WALTER A. ANDERSON
Content Editor

Contents

CHAPTER I

The Dimensions of Adult Education

Adult education is difficult to describe and almost impossible to define because it is found in so many different forms under the sponsorship of such a wide variety of institutions and agencies. This complex situation inclines any definition to be either too inclusive or too narrow. In general, the term *adult education* is used to designate all those educational activities that are designed specifically for adults. This perception of adult education is inclusive, but it does not extend to all those situations or activities in which learning by adults may occur.

Learning by adults may occur in two types of settings, but only one of these is properly identified as *adult education.* Adults may learn from their *natural societal setting*—everyday experiences in living, whether at work or at leisure. Adults can learn by reading, by watching television, from conversation, or by participation in the life of the community. By and large, however, such activities produce learning largely by chance or by accident. While everyday activities may provide unparalleled opportunities, the learning achieved thereby is casual and undirected as well as inefficient and uncertain. The intensity of the motivation to learn determines the nature and extent of the learning achieved. In some fairly rare instances an adult may be so strongly motivated that he achieves a high order of learning through self-education, by utilizing the opportunities provided in this natural societal setting. But although the natural societal setting provides opportunities to learn, it also contains distractions that inhibit learning. Too few adults learn enough sufficiently well in such a setting to satisfy either basic individual or societal needs for continuous learning.

The second setting in which learning by adults occurs is the *formal instructional setting,* in which the element of chance is minimized. This setting comes into being when an educational agent designs a sequence of tasks using specific learning procedures to help an adult achieve a mutually agreeable learning objective. This is adult education. In most instances, the ways in which it operates and the various auspices under which it is conducted differ so widely from the traditional "school" concept of education that it is not always recognized for what, in fact, it is.

Educational activities for adults may include the program at a Parent-Teachers Association or luncheon club meeting, a correspondence course, an in-service training program, a study discussion group, a public forum, or an evening class in a high school or university. These may be provided by public or private schools and colleges, public or volunteer health and welfare agencies, churches, businesses, industrial establishments, private clubs, proprietary schools, or the armed forces.

Whatever the form, content, duration, physical setting, or sponsorship, an activity is identified as adult education when it is part of a systematic, planned, instructional program for adults.

Scope

Adult education is both a means and an end in itself. As a means, it provides the instrument through which an agency can achieve a specific learning objective that has been determined to be essential to the successful accomplishment of the purposes of that agency. In such instances the education of the general adult population is of no importance; the program is directed and limited to the group involved in the purposes of the sponsoring agency. This is illustrated by the many in-service educational programs conducted for employees by businesses, the armed forces, volunteer agencies, or educational institutions. Such programs are designed to help this selected clientele keep abreast of vital changes in social conditions or in pertinent technology. The content is generally of limited interest to those not immediately involved and the administration of such programs is solely the concern of the sponsoring agent.

These purely private programs of adult education far outnumber public programs; however, accurate data for comparison are not available. Private programs are so complex and widely scattered that adequate data are difficult to collect. The absence of such data restricts the perception of adult education to those activities designed for the public in general. Thus no complete measure of the real extent of adult education is possible. Certainly there is far more adult education going on than even the most astute students of the field can estimate.[1]

The readily visible phase of adult education is that provided under the auspices of recognized educational institutions. These programs are an example of adult education as an end in itself. They are available to the public at large and the sponsoring institution is interested only in the general education of the public and in meeting individual and social needs for continuous learning.

Public programs of adult education are offered by most public school systems and universities and some private ones. The content of such programs is as varied as individual interests in learning; their emphasis range from hobbies and personal development to occupational and public affairs. The cost of public programs is shared by the participants and the sponsoring institution. In the case of public agencies, tax funds provide some of the support to a degree determined by the social utility or necessity of the programs they offer. Thus, fundamental and citizenship education tends to be wholly tax-supported while personal development or leisure subjects are usually largely self-sustaining. Private educational institutions tend to depend upon self-supporting activities because they are not eligible for tax support and because they will not subsidize their budget for normal activities. The concept of public responsibility for continuing education has not yet been accepted completely by society so there is no standard procedure with respect to financial support.

Most of what is written about adult education centers on these public programs since they are visible and, therefore, more readily available for study. Only recently have the private programs been subjected to analysis in such works as those of Clark and Sloan, which study adult educational activities in industrial and retail establishments.[2]

Need

The education of adults has constituted an integral part of all cultures at all times in history. It was so much a part of a culture that

---

[1] See *Handbook of Adult Education in the United States,* edited by Malcolm S. Knowles (Chicago: Adult Education Association, 1960).

[2] Harold F. Clark and Harold S. Sloan, *Classrooms in the Factories* (New York: New York University Press, 1958).

there is little specific historical data to provide a measure of its importance in earlier civilizations.[3] No social machinery specifically for the education of adults was necessary until cultures grew so complex that normal processes for continuing education were no longer adequate. It is only within the last several centuries that adult education has begun to emerge as an identifiable element. Recent history has produced a number of great episodic movements of adult education, ranging from literacy programs to lecture series. Some episodes resulted in the establishment of permanent institutional programs of adult education, while others are marked by short-lived but intensive activity. Each form of adult education developed to meet a particular need at a given moment in a manner dictated by the conditions at that time. As the nature of the need or of the conditions changes, the form also must change. When a particular form of adult education no longer serves a useful purpose, it must be replaced by a new form.

The perception of need and the resultant forms of adult education change from one era to another. In the seventeenth and eighteenth centuries the purpose of adult education centered around the idea of amelioration. Lower-class adults were taught to read the Bible in order to improve their morality and to help them accept their lot. This charity concept survives in many phases of adult education today. In the nineteenth century organized adult education attracted the better educated and aimed to satisfy curiosity about the unfolding world of scientific phenomena. In the early part of the twentieth century the central theme was an effort to raise the minimum educational level of an adult population which had been deprived of educational opportunity in youth. Although all these themes persist, the dominant theme at present is that of adjustment: to help adults learn to accommodate the rapid technical and social changes so characteristic of our time.

As the perception of need has altered, so have the forms of adult education. Some have persisted and survived; others have become extinct. In every instance the form has been determined by the social milieu in which it appeared. The charity schools of the eighteenth and nineteenth centuries have persisted, although their pur-

[3] Cf. C. Hartley Grattan, *In Quest of Knowledge* (New York: Association Press, 1955), and Thomas Kelly, *A History of Adult Education in Great Britain* (Liverpool: The University Press, 1962).

poses and sponsorship have changed.[4] They survive today in the ever-expanding night schools operated by local school systems which offer such a variety of educational programs that they have little in common with their predecessors. The lyceum of the nineteenth century [5] and the chautauqua of the twentieth century [6] have all but vanished from the scene; however, distantly related variants of these and other early forms survive today. The variety of forms which it has assumed complicates any historical analysis of adult education. Such an analysis illustrates, however, the persistence of the concept of continuing education and provides clues to the identification of the many forms which exist today.

Since the need for continuous education is an universal cultural trait, it is possible to identify some of the persistent social forces that have given rise to it.[7]

The expansion of knowledge. Human culture expands at an ever-increasing rate. Man's knowledge about himself and his world accumulates faster than his ability to absorb and use it. As a result, the sheer bulk of what can or must be known in any single branch of knowledge becomes unmanageable. The mastery of multiple branches of knowledge becomes impossible. This dilemma has encouraged specialization—mastery of a subject area in depth within ever-narrowing limits. Every man, therefore, becomes a specialist in some sense. Thus, every man comes to face two fundamental problems. First, if an individual keeps within the narrow limits of his own specialization, he quickly loses touch with the real world about him and is unable to participate intelligently with others in the management of his environment. Furthermore, his own specialized knowledge becomes obsolete within a period of from five to twenty years unless he acquires new knowledge continuously. Therefore, each person faces the task of constantly expanding the horizons of both his specific and his general knowledge.

With so much known and with so much more to be learned, every individual faces the certainty of becoming "obsolete" both as a specialist and as a member of human society unless he continuously

---

[4] *Ibid.*, pp. 65–76.

[5] Carl Bode, *The American Lyceum* (New York: Oxford University Press, 1956).

[6] Joseph E. Gould, *The Chautauqua Movement* (Albany, N.Y.: State University of New York, 1961).

[7] Cf. Wilbur C. Hallenbeck, "The Function and Place of Adult Education in American Society," *Handbook of Adult Education, op. cit.*, pp. 30–36.

engages in learning. Such continuous learning is not easy and cannot be left to chance. Because of the complexity of knowledge, few individuals can judge for themselves what is significant and timely, nor can they afford the uncertainty and inefficiency of self-education. Since the task of continuous learning is beyond the possibility of unguided individual achievement, society as a whole must assume the responsibility for the promulgation and use of adult educational opportunities. The adult education enterprise, in turn, is responsible —through the selection of content and the design of effective learning experiences—for the appropriateness and efficiency of the education it provides.

The enormity of technological developments. One principal result of the growth of knowledge is a corresponding growth of technological innovations. These innovations exert a major influence over the vocational life of an individual. They have changed the nature of work by rendering old skills obsolete while creating a need for new occupational skills. This change necessitates a different perception of the function and method of prevocational education. Rather than acquire specific skills, individuals must master the process of learning a complex of skills in specific vocational areas so that adjustment to future technological change can be accomplished with a minimum of personal displacement. The specific skills learned in youth become obsolete by middle age and few skills can be expected to survive through the productive life of an individual. Therefore, most workers must anticipate the need to learn new vocational skills to replace earlier skills rendered obsolete by technological change. Such new learning cannot be achieved by chance; society must make provisions for systematic education to assure optimum productivity.

Technological innovations also reduce the amount of time and human labor needed to produce the goods required by society. This creates expanding periods of leisure, and increased leisure provides more time for personal growth and development as well as greater opportunities to assume an active role in the social and political life of the society. Yet few individuals are adequately prepared to make effective use of their increased leisure. Therefore, systematic educational opportunities are essential if leisure is to become a contributory force in the development of society.

The complexity of social change. Both the advancement of knowledge and the subsequent technological innovations culminate in massive changes in the everyday life of the individual. They exert an ever-widening influence on social relationships, on patterns of behavior, and on the overall structure and organization of society. Every technological change, regardless of how minor it may appear, will eventually induce some alteration in established customs and habits. Major innovations, such as the automobile, induce penetrating social changes that have an impact upon every facet of life. This impact necessitates continuous change in basic human values, attitudes, and established beliefs. To bring about modifications in these sensitive areas, it is necessary to understand the cause of and necessity for change, as well as its nature and direction. Since such changes occur continuously, the learning necessary to adapt to them must also be continuous.

The impact of these persistent social forces at any given moment has varied in intensity. Consequently, the development of adult education has been marked by periods of intense interest and participation followed by periods of reduced activity. Certain forms of adult education, therefore, have loomed up more impressively than others, prompting some to attach values to these forms that are in reality reflections of the conditions in which it arose.

The alternating waves of public interest and disinterest, however, are marked by a general trend toward persistently increasing interest and participation. The low points in periods of lessened interest never reach the lowest points of earlier periods of decline. By the same token, the high points of involvement in adult education always rise above the peaks of earlier periods. Thus, interest in adult education never permanently diminishes nor has it yet achieved the maximum potential that might be anticipated.

Negative Forces

At the same time certain cultural forces stimulate adult education, other forces are acting to discourage or retard its development. These negative forces are found both in society and within the adult education enterprise itself.

The attitude toward education. Although society as a whole recognizes the value of education, many elements in society have an adverse attitude toward it. This is illustrated by the derision directed at "egghead" intellectuals and by the high rate of dropout from formal school programs. Such ambivalence creates a social climate that both encourages and retards participation in adult education programs. Whenever a society places a high value on education, the development of that society is furthered. English society in the nineteenth century placed a very high value on education, and this prompted the uneducated working class to form the Workers' Education Association.[8] As a result of the interest in education, the noted Oxford Conference of 1908 created the tutorial class scheme for the education of workers.[9] The workingmen of the time were encouraged to commit themselves to a three-year study program and the faculty of Oxford were persuaded to provide the instruction. This could not have occurred if the social climate had not stimulated an interest in education.

The opposite influence is noted in the destiny of the Correspondence Societies in eighteenth century England. These societies were small study-discussion groups made up largely of illiterate workingmen interested in improving their lot. The groups grew out of the concepts of freedom stimulated by the American Revolution and thrived on the ideas of Thomas Paine, whose pamphlets they read and discussed. But the social climate at that time resisted the spread of education. Because these groups dealt with ideas deemed to be reserved for the educated, they were declared subversive and outlawed by the government. Thus, when a society opposes education it retards its own growth. The history of adult education reflects the impact of different attitudes toward education in general and toward education for adults in particular.

Attitudes about the nature of education. Many people hold the notion that education is a state of being rather than of becoming, that they may terminate their education when they reach a state of self-determined sufficiency with respect to learning. This terminal concept of education is reinforced by such devices as grades, graduation, diplomas, and degrees—even though these provide no measure of either individual or social need for learning. With such an attitude, individuals are disinclined to seek further opportunities

[8] Mary Stocks, *The Workers' Educational Association* (London: George Allen & Unwin, 1953).

[9] *Oxford and Working-class Education* (Oxford: The University Press, 1908; reprinted 1951).

for systematic study and society is dissuaded from providing extensive opportunities for continuing education. In time, the concept of continuity of education will replace that of termination.

Another aspect of the concept of education is found in the recognition (or lack of it) of the wide variety of activities with a high educational potential in which adults participate. Formal schooling has so dominated the educational concept in modern society that few people utilize the many educational opportunities that exist outside the traditional school concept. It is only through the study of adult education that the full array of educational resources in the society become visible and their educational value recognized.

The institutionalization of adult education. As adult education develops, it tends to become institutionalized, and—in the manner characteristic of all social institutions—it comes to attach greater value to form than to function. The management and maintenance of the institution take precedence over the functions which the institution is intended to perform. This institutionalization tends to block the modification and adaptation of adult education to the changing requirements and conditions that grow out of a continually changing society. When such resistance persists, the institution becomes obsolete and can no longer fulfill its function. New institutions must come into existence. This process contributes to the episodic nature of adult education which, coupled with other negative influences, tends to present a dismal prognosis for consistency in the development of continuing education.

Institutionalization is counteracted, in part, by the growth of specialized knowledge about adults as individuals, about the learning process, and about the design and management of educational programs for adults. Such specialization contributes to greater efficiency and encourages the extension of education for adults into every facet of life.

Functions

The social forces and factors that create the need for continuous learning help to identify the functions of adult education and, in so doing, help to differentiate it from other more familiar forms of education.[10]

---

[10] See also Lyman Bryson, *Adult Education* (New York: American Book Company, 1936), pp. 29–48; and Hallenbeck, *op. cit.*, pp. 36–38.

Expansional. Individuals enter into adult life with various degrees of competence for the tasks which adulthood imposes. No individual is ever fully equipped for all the responsibilities of adult life; therefore, he must acquire new knowledge and skills continuously as his responsibilities develop and change through the years. Thus, as each stage of life expands the range of personal responsibility, adult education helps an individual to expand his competence from those skills involved in a vocation or profession to those involved in being a spouse, a parent, or a citizen.

Participational. A democratic society demands the informed participation of its members in the processes of government. This participation calls into play a variety of skills and knowledge not normally acquired by individuals through ordinary educational channels. Adult education provides access to knowledge pertinent to local, national, and international issues as well as training and practice in the skills of civic participation.

Integrational. In a lifetime of living in society, individuals accumulate a vast store of information and knowledge about a great range of subjects. Most of the problems which plague individuals could be resolved through the application of the knowledge they already possess. To do this, however, they must learn to integrate knowledge with experience in order to identify what must yet be learned and so that new knowledge will have meaning with respect to what is already known. The inability to identify the need for new learning is the greatest barrier to personal growth. Through systematic adult education, individuals can learn to identify their educational needs and to master the intellectual process that will enable them to integrate knowledge and apply it to the resolution of recurring problems.

Personal. Maturation is a lifelong process that requires continuous learning as an integral part of living and growing. Such learning will free the individual from ignorance, from obsolete attitudes and values, and from irrational or immature behavior. Adult education provides access to learning through which an individual achieves continuous growth toward maturity in all phases of life.

Institutions

In order to fulfill the functions of adult education, every institution and agency in the society is called into play in one way or another. Unlike pre-adult education, the continuing education of adults is not the responsibility of any one agency or group of agencies that can be readily identified as adult education institutions. This lack of centralized responsibility and its associated authority is simultaneously a strength and a weakness of the adult education enterprise. It is a weakness because the absence of clearly identified responsibility and authority mitigates against systematic planning and development to insure that all the various adult educational needs are met. As a strength, however, it tends to retard institutionalization so that adult education is better able to make the rapid adjustments in content, method, and organization that are necessary if it is to fulfill its functions effectively.

In the absence of any centralized authority, the responsibility for adult education is dispersed throughout the society. It is shared by every social institution in varying degrees; however, not every institution acknowledges or willingly accepts its share. Some institutions and agencies recognize this responsibility and interpret it as a responsibility for the education of the general adult population. Other institutions, on the other hand, become involved in adult education solely to achieve limited objectives that further the self-interest of the institution itself and have only indirect relation to the educational needs of individuals or of the society.[11]

In view of the varying degrees of involvement in adult education, it is possible to identify institutions and agencies with respect to their relationship to the total adult education enterprise.

Institutions for which adult education is the primary function. There are no institutions concerned solely with the education of adults which are common to all cultures. Institutions that have adult education as their primary function do exist in particular communities. One such is the Junto in Philadelphia, which was founded by Benjamin Franklin in the eighteenth century and still survives in modified form. The various Workingmen's Colleges, such as Birkbech College in England, fit into this category but op-

---

[11] See *Handbook of Adult Education in the United States, op. cit.*, p. 565, for a list of national organizations in adult education.

erate solely on the local community level. The Folk Schools of Scandinavia are also of this type, and although they tend to be universal in the Scandinavian countries, they have not spread successfully or extensively beyond that geographic area.

Certain agencies that exist solely for adult education are also confined to particular countries. In Canada, the Frontier College provides educational opportunities for men in isolated mining and lumber camps but does not provide for other adults. In the United States can be found the Foundation for Continuing Education and the Great Books Foundation, both of which were established to promote special kinds of adult education somewhat limited in method and content.

Institutions for which adult education is an extension of the primary function. There are many institutions and agencies whose primary function does not involve adult education but which have extended their functions to include programs of adult education. In general, such institutions are already involved in education in some form (as in the case of schools, universities, or libraries). In most instances, such institutions conduct their normal activities during the day and, in response to demands from the adult population, they have extended their activities into the evening to permit adult participation. This extension of normal daytime activities to include adult education has been achieved with some reluctance on the part of the institutions concerned. It necessitates considerable realignment of the concept of education and the development of new and different patterns of organization, a new methodology, and a new content orientation suited to the more mature level of the adult participant. Such necessary adjustments are not accomplished easily because institutional traditions and self-images tend to be inflexible and immutable.

Few of the established institutions included in this classification have achieved a truly functional educational program for adults, for they tend to transfer existing concepts to times convenient to the adult rather than create specific programs and services for the adult students. Existing patterns and regulations tend to block the development of adult-oriented education. The question of credit, for example, is such a barrier. Established educational institutions attach values to their patterns of organization, content, and methodology rather than to the quality of the educational experience they provide.

Consequently, it is difficult to introduce different patterns better suited to adult needs. Although such institutions now provide extensive opportunities for adult education, these barriers tend to inhibit the development of truly adequate programs conducive to extensive participation by adults. To a considerable extent, this control of the educational process by traditionalism at the expense of functionalism has contributed to the spread of adult education into the entire institutional structure of society and has retarded the establishment of a more nearly centralized and coordinated adult education enterprise.

The major institutions in this category are the library, the elementary and secondary school systems, junior or community colleges, and institutions of higher learning. The library is one of the major resources for learning in the natural societal setting and has recently increased its efforts to establish formal instructional settings for learning as a recognized phase of its responsibility. In this effort, libraries tend to concentrate on lecture series and study-discussion groups that emphasize the use of the library's resources.

An increasing number of public school systems across the nation (along with many private and parochial schools as well) are developing evening schools for adults. This extension of function began in the latter half of the nineteenth century in a few selected urban centers and has since spread to other urban areas as well as to some rural school districts. Originally these evening programs closely paralleled the day programs, providing equivalency education on the elementary and secondary level. These programs were stringently controlled so as to be equivalent in a very real sense. In recent years, however, vocational, general interest, and leisure education have been added, with considerable modification of the pattern and structure of the traditional programs. In some areas, day programs for adults are developing at an encouraging rate and increasing interest is being shown in planning activities and methods fitted to adult needs and interests.

The quantity and quality of education for adults provided by school systems varies widely from one system to another but, in general, such programs appear to be influenced more by expediency and popularity than by systematic educational planning. The principal barrier to public school adult education is found in the school system itself: school personnel tend to look upon the evening adult program as an unimportant and undesirable activity imposed upon them. At the same time, the most encouraging trend is the growing acceptance of the concept of continuing education as a public responsibility by citizens and by many enlightened professional and political school officials. Public school adult education will really come into its own when this concept permeates the entire school system and the community.

Junior colleges bridge the gap between public schools and institutions of higher education and display many of the best and worst features of both. Their role and responsibility as an educational force is neither clearly identified nor accepted by those involved; consequently, the adult education programs they conduct tend to duplicate the day program and to be haphazard and indeterminate rather than clearly defined and systematically ordered. Yet evening enrollment usually exceeds the day enrollment in most institutions.

Colleges and universities have been active in adult education longer than any other of the educational institutions. At the same time, their adult programs are more closely bound by tradition and thereby less functionally oriented to adult needs for higher education. The University Extension idea started at Cambridge University in England in the third quarter of the nineteenth century. Originally a lecture series, it has since expanded into a wide variety of activities. Those Extension programs unrelated to degrees or credits tend to be geared to adult needs and interests, thereby reflecting freer and more imaginative educational planning.

University extension divisions operate both credit and noncredit programs and employ a variety of methods—including correspondence, classes, workshops, forums, and residential activities. These are conducted on campus or in centers conveniently situated for the adults being served by them. Over the years, university extension education has grown—both in the number of adults involved and in the breadth of the program. Not every extension program enjoys the full support of its parent institution and economic considerations tend to determine the nature of university adult education.

Institutions for which adult education is a means of achieving a primary function. There are many institutions and agencies in society which are created to meet a need that may or may not be related to education. Ultimately, they come to depend upon adult education in order to achieve their primary purposes. These agencies may be private or governmental and they may be concerned with the production of goods or the provision of services.

By far the largest segment of the adult education enterprise fits into this category. Business and industry, for example, are the largest single consumers of adult education. At one time they depended upon existing educational resources to meet their need for educational opportunities but these proved incapable of providing the immediate functional training required. As a result, industry has developed its own job-related training.

Accurate data respecting the extent of adult education in business and industry are not available; however, Harold Clark has estimated that some five million employees take part in some kind of industry-sponsored education annually.[12] He estimates the expenditure for such education at around $10 billion annually, which is twice as much as the total public and private expenditure on higher education. It is obvious that the commercial enterprise recognizes the value of and necessity for continuing education with an intensity that has not yet permeated other phases of national life.

Governmental agencies on the local, state, and national level not only operate the public school systems but are also deeply involved in adult education in a variety of ways. This agency involvement in adult education fits into the present category because education is a supplemental function which is utilized to further the primary objectives of the agency concerned.

The armed forces operate extensive educational programs for service personnel. These programs are aimed at providing continuous military training and furthering the personal development of individual members.[13] It has been estimated that expenditures for armed forces education exceed the entire national budget for elementary education. Although most military training is confined to the military establishment, the armed forces also support educational programs developed cooperatively with civilian institutions. Many universities have developed special degree programs for military personnel and carry on extension classes on military establishments. In some cases the costs are shared by the federal government,

[12] Clark and Sloan, *op. cit.*

[13] Cyril O. Houle, *et al.*, *The Armed Services and Adult Education* (Washington, D.C.: American Council on Education, 1947).

the individual, and the university. In addition, the Armed Forces Institute offers correspondence courses to military personnel and the reserve components operate extensive educational programs in localities for the reserve force. Obviously, the first task of the services is to provide military training; however, they have broadened their concept of appropriate studies to include virtually any legitimate educational task.

Another governmental program of sizable proportions is that conducted by the Cooperative Extension Service of the United States Department of Agriculture.[14] The cost of this program is shared equally by the federal, state and local governments. The Extension Service operates in almost every county in the country and is concerned primarily with the improvement of agricultural production and the enrichment of rural life. With the decline in rural population, the Extension Service now operates in urban areas as well as rural; consequently, the nature of its program is changing. Where extension education was originally almost wholly vocational, it now includes activities aimed at broadening the horizons of rural people and establishing among them a better understanding of their relationship to the world at large. The effectiveness of the Extension Service in changing the character of rural life and agricultural productivity is nothing short of phenomenal, and provides an object lesson in the value of systematic education for adults. In something like seven years, for example, it revolutionized the production of corn in Iowa through the introduction of hybrid corn varieties.[15] In addition to operating effective educational programs, the Cooperative Extension Service has contributed extensively through research to the development of the science of adult education. No single facet of the adult education enterprise can claim with equal justification to have educated so many adults so well.

Public libraries are an essential arm of adult education for they provide the materials for education to other programs. Although organized educational activities for adults are not a major aspect of library service, they are growing in importance. Some libraries offer regular programs designed to emphasize such library resources

---

[14] Edmund de S. Brunner and E. Hsin Pao Yang, *Rural America and the Extension Service* (New York: Teachers College, Columbia University, 1949).

[15] Herbert F. Lionberger, *Adoption of New Ideas and Practices* (Ames, Iowa: Iowa State University Press, 1960).

as book reviews, recorded concerts, lecture series, and study-discussion groups. The Readers' Advisory Service, available in many public libraries, is a useful counseling service for adults that can put them in touch with appropriate educational resources in the community. Library-centered adult education is expanding rapidly in keeping with the growing interest in continuing education.

Health and welfare services (both public and private) depend heavily upon adult education to further their objectives. Good health, for example, is as much a matter of individual learning as it is a public responsibility. Health services have cleverly blended treatment and educational programs on an individual and group basis through maternity classes, well-baby clinics, sanitation, and similar health matters. Through extensive educational activities for adults, such services strive to improve public knowledge and sensitivity to those matters related to general health and welfare and devote about one third of their annual budgets to education.

CHAPTER II

The Adult

Adult education involves many different kinds of people with varying abilities, interests, motives and socioeconomic characteristics. Participation in adult education is influenced by factors that are components of both the personality and the social group life of the individual. These factors exert a profound influence upon the form, content, and character of the educational activity. In addition, they accentuate and explicate the fundamental distinctions between adult and pre-adult education.

Personal Characteristics

There are a number of factors influencing participation in adult education that, for convenience, are discussed here as personal characteristics since they reside almost exclusively within the adult as a person. These factors are not necessarily discrete and in most instances the influence and effect of any one factor is related to and interacts with every other as well as with those factors discussed later as social characteristics. Included among personal characteristics are such things as physiological changes, learning ability, motivation, attitudes, and interests.

Physiological changes. The adult organism undergoes continuous change as age advances. These biological alterations include sensory decline; loss in strength; lengthening of reaction time; decline in sexual capacity; changes in skin texture, muscle tone, and hair color; and a general decline in overall energy. Such physiological changes occur gradually and at different rates among individuals yet the overall general trend is constant. Most adults are unaware of this physical change until some traumatic experience forcefully accentuates it. For many adults physical vigor is a highly valued trait and awareness of decline may alter the adult's self-concept. Furthermore, these changes may induce an adult to underestimate his power to learn or to perform tasks, and this underestimation may be reflected in changes in interests and motivation.

The decrement in *visual acuity* may be one of the most obvious physiological changes observed by an adult and it is certainly one which has a direct effect upon the management of adult learning. The peak of visual acuity is reached some time between twenty and twenty-five years of age. From that point there is a slight but persistent decline until about forty to forty-five years of age, when it takes a sharp drop and continues at a steeper rate of decline throughout the balance of the life span. This change has its most noticeable affect upon reading, since the near-point of vision moves progressively further away until reading glasses become essential. Many adults are unwilling to admit to the need for glasses and this further hampers their feeling of confidence in a learning situation. The responsiveness of the eye to illumination decreases, as does the muscle power, so that close work such as reading becomes increasingly difficult.

Such changes in visual acuity necessitate different approaches to learning as age advances. Adult students need stronger illumination to compensate for changes in the ability of the eye to admit light. They need increasingly larger sizes of print and sharper contrasts in color. Furthermore, they cannot read as much in a given amount of time in the middle and later years as they could earlier; therefore, the reading expectation must be reduced. Thus, in formal adult night classes or discussion groups, shorter rather than longer reading assignments are indicated.[1]

Audio acuity declines in the same way as vision does, with the added impact that attitude toward hearing will have on comprehension. Although an adult may be able to perceive sound, he may not comprehend its meaning, and this comprehension is influenced by his own perception of his ability to hear. Obviously, the decline in this facility is an important barrier to learning and imposes upon the instructional agent the responsibility of compensating for hearing loss. This can be achieved by well-modulated voice control; by always facing the group so that those who unconsciously supplement sound with lip-reading can see what is said; and by supplementing

[1] Samuel E. Hand, *A Review of Physiological and Psychological Changes in Aging and Their Implications for Teachers of Adults,* 3rd ed., Bulletin 71G-1 (Tallahassee, Fla.: State Department of Education, April, 1957), pp. 2–5.

oral instruction with visual aids (such as writing unfamiliar words or terms on the blackboard).[2]

Homeostatic adjustment describes the ability of the body to maintain a constant internal temperature although external conditions may vary. This adjustment changes with age as the body loses its ability to maintain internal temperature; therefore, as age advances, adults cannot adjust to external conditions easily and cold or drafts can become barriers to learning. This is particularly significant when the members of the instructional group vary widely in age or when the age of the instructor is decidedly less than that of the group members.

The overall *loss in energy* that increases with age influences the adult's ability and willingness to participate in educational programs. The energy requirements of his vocational life may be so high that there is little energy left for taxing educational tasks. This necessitates adjustments in the form and nature of the educational task in order that its energy requirement is not prohibitive in terms of the energy available.

Physiological changes often create the need to erect defenses against losses. These defenses may be manifested in limited choices, in an intolerance for ambiguity whereby a rigid structure is forced on the environment, or in the assumption of extreme positions without apparent justification. The content of the learning situation, as well as the instructional processes or the organizational pattern, can achieve hostile responses which may result in avoidance or even in total withdrawal. Instructional agents must be sensitive to individual members of a learning group so as to avoid or diminish the threats that are naturally present in every situation. Helping the adult participant to recognize and understand the effects of age is one way of diminishing the threatening nature of education. Time expectations must be reduced to compensate for physiological changes. Thus, the material or educational experience that might be covered in a month with a pre-adult group may take two months or more as the age of the learning group advances.[3]

Learning ability. There are sharp differences of opinion with respect to the nature and extent of the changes in learning ability that occur with age. There is a general agreement that the peak of

[2] *Ibid.*, pp. 5–7.
[3] *Ibid.*, pp. 7–12.

learning ability is reached somewhere between twenty and twenty-five years of age. Beyond this point, however, there is no clear-cut perception of learning ability in the adult. In his early studies of adult learning, E. L. Thorndike concluded that after the peak there was a decline in learning ability of approximately one per cent per year up to about age forty-two, following which the rate of decrement accelerated.[4] In a re-study and extension of Thorndike's earlier work, Lorge concluded that adults were penalized by time as age advanced and that although the amount of *time* required for learning increased with age, the *power* to learn did not decline significantly from its peak.[5] Weschler, on the other hand, tends to support Thorndike by insisting that both time and power change and that loss in learning ability with age is greater than Lorge assumes.[6] Further research will be needed before the dispute is resolved; nevertheless, there is nothing in existing research knowledge to support the old saw that "you can't teach an old dog new tricks."

Whatever the change in learning ability after the peak period may be, ability itself is less significant in adult learning than a variety of other factors. Physiological changes impose certain limitations on learning, particularly with respect to the element of *time* (as Lorge discovered). Both Thorndike and Lorge tend to agree that any adult can learn almost anything he wants to learn at any age about as well as he could have learned it at his peak of learning ability—if he allows sufficient time for learning and does not expect to learn as fast as he did previously.

Previous experience with learning appears to influence adult learning appreciably. The more experience in learning new material an individual has had, the greater will be the facility with which he can attack new learning tasks. Furthermore, the greater the intellectual endowment and the greater the amount of education, the less sharp is the decline in learning ability. Continuous intellectual activity through creative imagination and continuous learning tends to retard the decline of mental abilities; thus, learning is

---

[4] E. L. Thorndike, *Adult Learning* (New York: The Macmillan Company, 1936), Chap. 12. See also W. C. Hallenbeck, ed., *Psychology of Adults* (Chicago: Adult Education Association, 1963).

[5] Irving Lorge, "Capacities of Older Adults," in *Education for Later Maturity*, edited by Wilma Donahue (New York: William Morrow & Co., Inc., 1955), pp. 36–59.

[6] David Weschler, *The Measurement and Appraisal of Adult Intelligence* (Baltimore: The Williams & Wilkins Co., 1958), Chap. 9.

the best cure for an adult's inability to learn. Occupation, too, affects ability to learn, for those adults active in occupations requiring the use of learned mental skills or intellectual activity tend to retain the use and ability of that material longer than those who have not used them continuously. An accountant or mathematician, for example, retains the ability to handle mathematical concepts longer and to learn new processes more easily than does a person whose occupation does not require the use of mathematical skills.[7]

A desire to learn and an interest in the material to be learned appear to exert a greater impact upon ability to learn than any other factors. Motivation and interest, therefore, are significant forces in learning, but these, too, alter with age.

Motivation. Motivation is goal-directed behavior which grows out of the needs of an individual at a specific point of time in a specific situation.[8] Motives may stem from the physical organism, in which case they are unlearned motives originating from organic needs, or they may stem from the social person, in which case they are learned motives that arise out of experience in living. The motives that lead to participation in adult education or to learning stem from the needs that arise out of experience. The nature, quality, and intensity of motivation is influenced by such factors as knowledge of the task, level of aspiration, previous experience, social role, and perception of education.

Social Role

An individual is called upon to assume many different roles in society as he passes through his life span. Each role produces a developmental task or tasks ". . . which must be filled within a limited time or presents itself suddenly and with urgency. . . ." [9] These tasks require new learning if they are to be performed adequately. Thus, at every stage in life there is a need for new learning to perform new developmental tasks that are created by the assumption of a new role in society.

Most of the education of youth is devoted to preparation to meet

[7] Edmund de S. Brunner *et al., An Overview of Adult Education Research* (Chicago: Adult Education Association, 1959), Chap. 2.

[8] Muzafer Sherif, *An Outline of Social Psychology* (New York: Harper & Row, Publishers, 1948).

[9] Brunner, *et al., op. cit.*, p. 37.

anticipated needs, often at the neglect of the specific developmental tasks that face the youth. Learning for the future is time-consuming and inefficient since the most teachable moments are those which immediately precede the need and, therefore, the use of the material learned.

Teachable moments occur when the amount of energy expended in fulfilling a particular social role is high and the individual is receptive to information directly related to the fulfillment of that role. Awareness of this need for learning provides the motivation for adult learning; adult education is, therefore, directed toward immediately practical objectives.

Social roles tend to fit into the life cycle patterns of individuals. They include being a spouse, a parent, a worker, a homemaker, a friend, a citizen, a church member, or any other of the complex of activities in which an adult becomes involved. Each role creates new developmental tasks and every adult needs new and specific learning, but not all adults are sufficiently aware of their need for learning to be motivated to participate in adult education.[10]

Levels of aspiration. An adjunct of the social role is the level of aspiration. This is the anticipated level of achievement with which each individual faces each new task. The level of aspiration is directly related to individual goals which, in turn, are related to the social role. As the social role changes, the goals also change which, in turn, alters the level of aspiration and, consequently, the nature and intensity of the motivation. An individual's goals may provide the motivation to participate in an educational activity while his level of aspiration provides the motivation that determines the amount and intensity of his learning. The greater the familiarity with learning, the higher the level of aspiration is apt to be.

Perception. In spite of the recognition of developmental tasks, of the identification of goals, or of the level of aspiration, an individual may not become involved in adult education unless he has a perception of the value of education. Education must be perceived, on the one hand, as having value for solving problems and, on the other hand, as the means to greater happiness and success. With these perceptions of education strengthening motivation, it is necessary that an individual be aware of the availability of a particular

---

[10] Robert Havighurst, "Social Roles of the Middle-Aged Person—A Method of Identifying the Needs of Adults," *Notes and Essays,* No. 4 (1953).

program or activity that will match his specific need. Furthermore, the particular agency providing the program, and the circumstances or conditions under which it is available, must be congenial to his own self-perception and predisposition if participation is to occur.

The task. With motivation providing the stimulus to participation in an educational activity, further and different motivation is required in order that such participation result in effective learning. This further strengthening of motivation is a result of the nature and management of the instructional situation. The specific learning task must be meaningful to the learner and related to his goals and level of aspiration. A knowledge of the task to be undertaken increases the efficiency with which it is accomplished. In other words, when an adult understands the purpose of the task, he increases his output.[11]

Associated with an understanding of purpose is awareness of progress. Knowledge that the results of performance of a task will be available and continuous awareness of those results tend to strengthen motivation and enhance increased performance. Such measurements of achievement should not be external to the learner, however. When an adult is compared with a superior group, such a comparison tends to lower the level of aspiration. Comparison with an inferior group, on the other hand, tends to raise the level of aspiration. But any comparisons among adults are odious and any measures of performance should be limited to successive measures of the individual's own performance.

The more meaningful the learning task is, the greater is the degree of ego-involvement in performance likely to be. Such ego-involvement in a task tends to generate a sustaining power that leads to successful achievement. To increase ego-involvement, therefore, the goals of the learning activity must be well defined and the anticipated difficulties or prospects of achievement clearly stated. This enables the learner to anticipate both difficulty and success so that he can make his own appraisal of achievement which strengthens his motivation.

The material learned in the task may influence the self-perception of the learner. There is no strictly neutral content in learning, since

[11] D. W. Chapman and J. Volkman, "Social Determinate of the Level of Aspiration," in *Readings in Social Psychology,* edited by T. M. Newcombe and E. L. Hartley (New York: Holt, Rinehart & Winston, Inc., 1947).

all content is both intellectual and emotional. An adult will guage the implications of the new knowledge in terms of its impact upon his own self-image and upon his relationship to his group. Thus, new material may have an implicit threat value which will decrease motivation to learn, or it may have reinforcement value that may strengthen motivation. Instructional agents must be sensitive to the practical objectives of adults and to the emotional impact new knowledge may have on them. This emphasizes the need to relate new learning to past experiences; where such a relationship may appear ambiguous, specific elements to achieve integration must be built into the design and conduct of the activity. The integration of new knowledge with past experience is an essential element in relating learning tasks to individual goals and tends to increase both ego-involvement in the learning task and to raise the level of aspiration so that motivation is continuously regenerative.[12]

Attitudes and interests. Attitudes and interests exert a profound affect upon an adult's involvement in further learning; however, both are, for the moment, imperfectly understood and inadequately handled by adult educators.

Attitudes. Attitudes may be defined as "... implicit drive-producing responses ..." which are formed in relation to objects, persons, or ideas.[13] They are not discrete units; they exist in a functional interdependence with other elements that compose the individual personality. Thus, they are functional expressions of personal values; they provide consistency to behavior, express identification with a social group, and reflect the internal reaction or response to experience.

Attitudes are learned and relatively stable; thus, they change only as a result of circumstances which are highly important to an individual. Because attitudes are a product of learning, they will differ systematically from one person to another, although individuals with comparable positions in the social structure are apt to have had similar experience and thus to have some attitudes in common.

By virtue of their nature, attitudes affect learning in a variety of different ways. They influence motivation to participate in adult

---

[12] Robert Havighurst and B. Orr, *Adult Education and Adult Needs* (Chicago: Center for the Study of Liberal Education for Adults, 1956).

[13] R. A. Sim, ed., *Canada's Farm Radio Forum* (Paris: UNESCO, 1954).

education in that they reflect the individual's perception of education. They influence goals and levels of aspiration in that they reflect personal and social values. They affect and, to some extent, control the actual learning achieved in that they determine the response to material encountered in the learning situation.

Just as attitudes influence learning, so may learning influence attitudes. As the individual advances in age, his attitudes tend to crystallize and to become immutable; however, since attitudes are learned, continuous learning throughout life can retard the process of attitude crystallization. It is imperative, therefore, that the instructional agent recognize the impact of the learning situation upon attitude formation in order to avoid those circumstances that may sponsor the creation or crystallization of negative attitudes toward content or the learning process itself. Every educational activity is a potential source of attitude formation or change, and the design and management of the learning situation will affect the attitudes that result. Attitude formation or change may itself be an instructional objective, so that both content and process are selected with respect to their influence on attitudes.[14]

Interests. Interests are somewhat akin to attitudes in that they cannot be identified precisely, are purely internal factors, and are subject to modification. As a term, *interests* identifies some factor within an individual which acts to cause him to be attracted to or repelled by something in his environment. The causative force is unknown; the reasons for the attraction or repulsion are unclear; and the precise influence of interest upon behavior is obscure.

Interests can be studied by observing the behavior that is presumed to result from or to reflect these interests. From such studies it is clear that interests are affected by age and are likely to change as age advances as a result of the physiological changes incident to aging. Younger adults tend to be more interested (i.e., more active) in pursuits involving physical effort (such as sports) or adventure (such as mountain climbing). As age advances and physiological changes set in, interests gradually shift from physical activities to activities which are more sedentary in nature.[15] This does not mean, however, that interests shift to intellectual pursuits in the later years,

[14] Brunner, *et al., op. cit.,* Chap. 4.

[15] E. K. Strong, *Change of Interests with Age* (Palo Alto, California: Stanford University Press, 1931).

but that they shift from physical pursuits. Substitute interests may or may not be developed. This change in the nature of interests may offer one explanation for the low participation rate of young adults in adult education programs.

Interests appear to be influenced also by formal educational levels. People with more education tend to be interested in higher intellectual material or unfamiliar content areas. Those with less education lean toward interest in activities that fall within the range of familiarity and which require less intellectual involvement. This, in part, explains the low participation rate of those with less formal education in the intellectually demanding adult education programs.

Occupation also affects interests. Adults, at least in the earlier years, tend to have greater interest in activities related to their occupation or vocation. This interest reflects the life goals of the individual. Since these goals change in the middle period of adult life, the interest of the individual also changes, shifting from vocationally related activities to other kinds of pursuits. In fact, interest in the vocation itself tends to decline as age advances. Individual goals influence interests in another way: adults striving for increased status will assume the interests characteristic of the group to which they want to belong.

Interests, like attitudes, can be changed. Usually some kind of provocation is necessary in order to develop new interests or widen existing interests. Adult education can provide such provocation, but if it is to do so, more than the content alone is involved. If the instructional situation in general provides a pleasurable experience, then interest in the content is apt to be aroused. Thus, the total social environment, as well as the specific instructional task, is pertinent to the development of interest.[16]

Social Characteristics

In addition to certain factors identified here as personal characteristics, there are a number of factors normally identified as socioeconomic characteristics that relate an individual to his social group. These characteristics tend to identify those adults who participate in further learning and to distinguish those who do not. Further-

---

[16] Brunner, *et al.*, *op. cit.*, Chap. 6.

more, there tends to be a relationship between the socioeconomic characteristics of participants and the kinds of institutional programs of adult education in which they become involved. Through a comparative analysis of such characteristics, therefore, it is possible to identify the kinds of people most apt to participate in specific kinds of programs.[17]

Socioeconomic. Participation in adult education is closely related to participation in the organized group life of the community, so that generalizations applicable to the one are equally appropriate for the other. Certain *socioeconomic status* measurements show a relation to participation. In urban communities, *occupation* appears to affect participation (with those in higher-status occupations tending to be more active). *Income,* which is determined by occupation, is a variable which indirectly affects participation. Naturally, it costs money to take part in educational activities; therefore, those with less money are less likely to become involved in adult education programs. *Educational level* is a variable directly related to occupation and income: those with more education are found to outnumber those with less education in the groups involved in adult education. This educational status differential is particularly marked in institutional programs. Universities, quite naturally, tend to draw the better educated while public schools tend to attract those with less education. Although this differential is not particularly important, it is significant to note that no programs reach the lowest educational levels where adult education is most needed. At any rate, it appears that adult education is widening the gap between the educated and the uneducated. In summary, these *socioeconomic* status variables indicate that the higher levels are more apt to participate in adult education and that particular institutional programs tend to draw from specific status groups.

Age as such is not a significant barrier to participation; however, adults at the extremities of the age continuum tend to participate less. Participation tends to be fairly high from the late twenties or early thirties to the early fifties. After fifty there is a gradual but continuous decline in participation. The public schools tend to draw more on the younger age groups than do other institutional programs. *Sex* is a factor in participation only in relation to age

[17] Coolie Verner and John S. Newberry, Jr., "The Nature of Adult Participation," *Adult Education,* Vol. 7 (Summer, 1958), 208–22.

and social status. Women from lower socioeconomic levels are least active; as social status increases, participation by women increases.

Marital status exerts some influence: married persons are generally more active participants than those who are either single or widowed. *Residence* has a decided influence, with rural areas showing more participation than urban areas; however, the differences are more qualitative than quantitative. Insofar as adult education is concerned, the higher population density of the urban area permits a wider variety of program offerings which tend to draw greater numbers of people than is possible in low-density rural areas. Distance from place of meeting, however, is not a significant factor as it was once thought to be. Repeated studies have shown that other factors discussed here tend to affect participation more than does distance. *Religion* is a factor with respect to nonchurch-related participation: Protestants tend to be more active than Catholics; among Protestants, the more formalized denominations tend to be better represented than the less formal sects.[18]

Institutional differences. The single most significant factor affecting participation is socioeconomic status. Of the indices of social status, educational level is by all odds the most significant variable. This is reflected not only in the form and institutional sponsorship of adult education, but also in the method and content of instructional activities. Table 1 points up the differences among various forms of adult education with respect to the various indices discussed.

Public school and junior college programs and correspondence courses attract more young adults than any other forms of adult education. This is due to the prevocational opportunities offered by those programs. The bulk of the participants in all programs fall between the ages of twenty to forty-four; only the Great Books and Home Demonstration programs show any considerable participation by adults above the age of forty-five. Very little is done by any program for the adult of sixty and over.

Comparisons among programs with respect to educational level of participants show a varied distribution. The public schools draw participants with nine years of school or more and the largest percentage have had some years of college work. This attraction stems

[18] Brunner, *et al.*, *op. cit.*, Chap. 6.

TABLE 1

Characteristics of Participants in Selected Adult Education Programs: Estimates Projected from Sample Studies(a)*

Characteristics(b)	General Population (Per Cent)	Public Schools	Junior Colleges	University Extension	Private Correspondence	Great Books	Home Demonstration(c)	All Class Activities(h)
		Per Cent of Enrollment				Per Cent of Members		Per Cent Reporting
Sex								
Male	49.1	— (d)	51.7	57	74.8	41	None	...
Female	50.9	—	48.3	43	25.2	59	100	...
Age								
15 to 19	10.0	6 (e)	12.8	9 (e)	20.2	None	None	6.1
20 to 29	22.5	45 (e)	36.5	45 (e)	43.9	16	14 (e)	23.0
30 to 44	31.1	33 (e)	36.8	35 (e)	28.8	41	35 (e)	41.5
45 to 59	18.3	14 (e)	} 14.6	10 (e)	6.4	26	40 (e)	23.1
60 and over	17.4	2		Negligible	.7	12	11 (e)	6.2
Not reported	.7	...	2.3	...	...	5	...	.1
Education Level								
0 to 4 years	10.8	2.0	2.1	None	None	None	Negligible	1.6
5 to 8 years	36.1	6.1(f)	15.1	} 5	12.9	2	22 (e)	...
9 to 11 years	17.0	13.1(f)	} 55.3		35.7	} 18	25 (e)	...
High School Graduate	20.2	15.8(f)		} 48	37.0		30 (e)	39.0
1 to 3 years College	7.2	39.1(f)	18.2		8.2	} 75	15 (e)	...
4 or more years College	6.0	24.6(f)	9.2	47	3.9		4 (e)	7.0
Not Reported	2.7	.1	.1	...	.3	5	3 (e)	52.3
Economic Status								
Low	22.4	2 (e)	4.5	Negligible	...	...	...	...
Below Average	16.2	26 (e)	16.4	20 (g)	...	...	...	...
Average	35.0	35 (e)	57.6 }		...	...	...	...
Above Average	19.9	25 (e)	17.3 }	70 (g)	...	...	...	...
High	6.6	12	4.2	10 (g)	...	...	...	...
Occupational Group								
Professional Technical	4.4	5.8	13.6	55	7.0	37	...	17.4
Managerial	4.5	} 17.8	5.9	8	3.3	8	...	2.8
White Collar	9.8		17.9	} 3	16.3	14	...	...
Skilled and semi-skilled	17.1	} 26.3	12.1		30.3	3	...	23.7
Unskilled and Service	8.2		14.4	Negligible	17.5	Negligible	...	2.8
Farmers	3.9	— (d)	9.2	5	1.7	None	...	2.0
Housewives	22.1	24.2	15.2	2	7.0	34	75	...
Others and Not Reported	30.0	25.9	21.7	...	16.9	4	25	42.9

Notes:

(a) Studies listed following each section in the text.

(b) U. S. Bureau of Census, *Characteristics of the Population, 1950.*

(c) Membership of Home Demonstration Clubs.

(d) Data from studies made in several areas not constant.

(e) Adjusted from data taken from studies showing minor variation.

(f) Data taken from studies in areas where the population differs significantly from the general population with respect to the characteristics shown.

(g) Interpolated from data not directly comparable.

(h) Based on the Sample Census as reported by Holden (17).

* Source: Coolie Verner and John S. Newberry, Jr., "The Nature of Adult Participation," *Adult Education,* Vol. VII (Summer, 1958), 215. Reprinted by permission of the Adult Education Association.

from the tremendous range of activities offered by the school system. Junior colleges tend to attract the person who has finished high school or who has had some years of college work. This may result from the fact that much of the evening program offered by such institutions is offered for credit. University extension programs draw their participants almost exclusively from the college-level population. Correspondence courses and Home Demonstration Clubs are heavily weighted toward those who may or may not have finished high school. The Great Books and study-discussion groups in general tend to draw largely from the college-level population, although some participants may not even have finished high school.

Barriers to participation. From various studies of participation it is clear that existing programs of adult education do not appeal to all segments of the adult population. Studies indicate that some 60 per cent of the population does not participate in the organized group life in a community. Certainly a substantial proportion of the adult population is not involved in institutional programs of adult education. These nonparticipants are likely to be over forty-five years of age and to have less than a high school education. They are probably from the lower socioeconomic levels, female, nonwhite, and rural residents. The same kinds of people who participate in adult education are found to be active in the formal community organizational life. The same kinds of people who do not participate in one, do not participate in the other.[19]

In spite of the low rate of participation in formal community organizations, there is a very high rate of participation in the informal community life, so a great deal of adult learning occurs independently of and apart from the organized programs of adult education. But our concern here is with the barriers to greater participation in adult education. The high rate of informal participation has interesting implications for adult education. It would seem to indicate, among other things, that the way to reach the uninvolved is through informality, for the less formal and more casual the structure of adult education is, the greater is the likelihood that it will appeal to the nonparticipant. This, of course, raises complex administrative problems since the development of informality would involve creating patterns of organization and operation outside the

---

[19] Alan Booth, "A Demographic Consideration of the Nonparticipant," *Adult Education,* Vol. XI (Summer, 1961), 223–29.

normal institutional framework. Furthermore, it would evoke a different conception of education than that which characterizes the institutional structure.

Inherent in adult education are a number of traditional patterns that are barriers to the greater extension and modification of the existing system.

1. Leadership for adult education comes from the parent institution so that it is preconditioned to established customs and mores respecting the nature and form of education. Thus, institutional patterns are self-perpetuating, and since the bulk of leadership in adult education is not specifically educated for it, the problem of introducing change into the structure is formidable.

2. The marginality of adult education with respect to the role and function of the parent institution makes any attempt to develop a truly functional program precarious. Such a program may jeopardize the whole concept of adult education as an institutional responsibility. A functional program of adult education specifically designed for the nonparticipant would differ so much from the recognized institutional pattern that it would be rejected by the parent body.

Massive and significant changes in the pattern of adult education are improbable; therefore, it is necessary to find other ways to involve the nonparticipant. Changes can be brought about within the existing structure that will not threaten the stability of the adult education program. These changes fall almost exclusively within the domain of the administrative and instructional agents. The format and content of a program can be geared more closely to the educational, social, and psychic needs of participants. Activities can be scheduled at the greater convenience of participants within the limits imposed by the institution. Instructional processes can be used that will increase involvement of the learner in the learning activity. Some program activities can be conducted in places more socially acceptable to the expected participants in order to overcome resistance to the institutional setting.

Although adult educators should look realistically at their programs in terms of the expected participants, they must also look elsewhere. Numerous research studies have pointed out the importance of informal opinion leaders who influence others in their personal day-to-day contacts. These are not formal leaders, nor do they necessarily hold positions of high social prestige. These opinion leaders tend to be the audience of mass media who then disseminate the information gathered to those whose opinion they influence. Such leaders are not readily identified; therefore, adult educators cannot work through them directly. By the judicious use of mass media, through which information can be diffused to opinion leaders as well as to potential participants, the importance of adult education can be amplified.[20]

In every area of the community there are those who are among the first to accept a new idea; those who wait until others have tried it; and those who never accept the idea at all. This is characteristic of response to adult education. Some of the potential participants will respond immediately to information about the availability of adult education programs. A much larger number will wait for further information about the program from friends and opinion leaders. The largest group will be those who never participate. It is on the first two groups that the adult educator must concentrate his attention in designing and using communication media. They are the ones who constitute the potential participants. There is little that can be done about the third group.

---

20 Elihu Katz and Paul Lazarsfeld, *Personal Influence* (New York: The Free Press of Glencoe, Inc., 1955).

CHAPTER III

The Adult Educator

Adult education is not a well-delineated professional field, although it is in the process of becoming so. There is no generally recognized role that can be tagged as unique to adult education, so there is no clearly defined preprofessional education and no specific line of career development. These characteristics of adult education differentiate it from all other educational systems in the society.

Adult education is a marginal activity that permeates the entire institutional structure of society; therefore, the adult education role is a marginal activity for the institutional representatives who assume it. Within every institution, the line of career development is linked to the dominant function of the institution; therefore, marginal functions such as adult education do not follow a separate career line. Thus, opportunities for personal advancement are not related to the adult education function and the position of adult educator becomes a stage in the progression from lesser to greater status and responsibility within the institutional framework. Adult educators are drawn from other positions in the institution and pass on to other, unrelated positions. In a typical school system, for example, a teacher aiming for advancement in the administrative area may move into an adult night school principalship either full-time or part-time to gain administrative experience. After a time, he will move into a day school principalship for which his background in adult education has served merely as training. The adult education job is not perceived by him or by his superiors as a specific career requiring specialized knowledge and skill and having its own line of development.

To some extent, the recognition of adult education as a specific career rests with those responsible for it. Those who perform the adult education role in an institution rarely perceive themselves as adult educators. They tend to identify themselves in terms of the primary function of the institution in which they are functioning as adult educators. Thus, the Readers' Advisor identifies himself as "a librarian"; the agricultural agent is "an agriculturist"; and the training director in industry is "a businessman in the management hierarchy." Because of this lack of self-perception and lack of unity within the adult education professional group, it is difficult to assess the number and characteristics of those engaged in adult education.

This state of affairs is changing. As the demand for continuous educational opportunities increases, it accents the need for more attention to be accorded the adult educational programs in institutions. This, in turn, creates the need for specialized personnel. At the same time, the discipline of adult education is advancing and graduate education for adult educators is being offered by more and more leading universities. Ultimately, these forces will result in a greater recognition of adult education as a specialized professional area of work and study.

Pyramid of Leadership

The identification of adult educators has been facilitated by the establishment of a typology of adult education leadership created by Professor Cyril O. Houle.[1] In this typology he has sorted out the classes of persons who provide leadership for adult education both quantitatively and qualitatively. The resulant distribution assumes the shape of a pyramid, with the volunteer leaders forming the broad base, part-time leadership the middle section, and full-time professional leadership the apex. This construction makes it easier to identify adult educators, to assess their roles and degrees of involvement, and to arrive at some perception of the extent of knowledge about educating adults.

Volunteer leadership. The broad base of Houle's leadership pyramid is composed of a vast number of individuals who act as adult educators on a voluntary basis. The exact number in this category cannot be estimated with any accuracy, for it includes members of every organization in the society. Their involvement in adult education varies and usually depends upon the nature of the responsibility which the individual volunteer assumes. The

[1] Cyril O. Houle, "The Education of Adult Educational Leaders," in *Handbook of Adult Education in the United States,* edited by Malcolm S. Knowles (Chicago: Adult Education Association, 1960), pp. 117–28.

efficiency and effectiveness of the ways in which the volunteer fulfills his responsibility depend to some extent upon his seriousness of purpose and upon the preparation which he acquires for the task.

The largest single group of volunteer adult educators is probably found among the program chairmen of the multitude of voluntary organizations which exist in every community in the land. This group rarely receives any specialized training for the task, although some organizations (such as the Parent-Teachers' Association or the General Federation of Women's Clubs) do offer some assistance to local units. This may take the form of prepackaged program materials or the occasional institute or workshop which offers training in the skills of program planning and management. Some organizations, such as the Associated Junior Leagues, specialize in the development of skilled volunteers. In such cases the purposes and programs of the organization are devoted to the education of volunteers for a variety of roles in the community—among them, adult education.

The selection, training, and use of volunteer adult educators has been developed systematically by the Cooperative Extension Service.[2] A county agent will select volunteer representatives from local neighborhoods for intensive training to perform specific adult educational tasks. These volunteers then pass on what they have learned to individuals or to small groups in their own neighborhoods. This careful, systematic program of volunteer education and use has extended the range and effectiveness of the county agents to include those who might not be influenced otherwise by the extension education program.

With volunteers forming the largest single block of adult educators, there is an urgent need for the systematic education of volunteers in the skills of adult education. In every case this would include training in the fundamental principles regarding the identification of educational needs, the design of suitable programs, and the management of instructional situations. Further research is needed into the requirements of specific volunteer positions in order to design and conduct appropriate training programs for particular

---

[2] Joseph L. Matthews, "The Cooperative Extension Service of the United States," in *Rural Social Systems and Adult Education* edited by Charles P. Loomis *et al.* (East Lansing, Mich.: The Michigan State College Press, 1953), pp. 51–80.

groups. This, of course, is the responsibility of professional adult educators.

Part-time leadership. This category, according to Houle, includes those who perform an adult education leadership role in addition to other duties for which they are paid by the institution or agency by which they are employed. Such part-time adult educators, like the volunteer leaders, are rarely trained or experienced in adult education. They tend to perform their tasks while they learn from experience by trial and error.

One large group in this category is composed of the many part-time adult leaders in evening extension and adult night school classes. Many of these teachers are regularly employed in the pre-adult day programs of the university or school system, but this is not necessarily an indication of skill or competence in the conduct of adult learning situations. The teaching of adults has many elements in common with teaching on the pre-adult level, but the differences between the two are greater than the similarities. Such teachers need training in adult education similar to that given to volunteers but with greater intensity and concentration on the fundamental principles of adult education.

All the many part-time leaders need the same core material about adult learning and the design and management of instructional activities for adults. In addition, they require specialized training appropriate to the particular adult education task which they perform. Thus, public health nurses, librarians, museum personnel, education officers in the armed forces, and social workers, among others, need to learn how to adapt and apply the basic principles of adult education to the peculiar situations they encounter in their different roles.

There is a growing trend toward the inclusion of advanced study in adult education as a part of the graduate curricula designed for persons in particular fields. Some of these part-time adult educators seek advanced degrees in the field of adult education itself. These trends promise to continue and to increase as the pressures for the expansion of educational opportunities for adults grow heavier.

Professional leadership. The apex of Houle's pyramid includes the specialists who are professional adult educators. These are the fewest in number but exercise the greatest influence on the development of adult education. Included in this group are the staffs of university extension programs, the agricultural extension service, public school adult education divisions, and similar specialists in a variety of institutions and agencies that take a significant part in the provision of opportunities for continuing education.

Not all such specialists are trained specifically in adult education, but the number trained is increasing steadily as these positions develop specific career lines so that individual's career expectations lie wholly within the field of adult education. Such professional training is usually at the master's level but increasingly at the doctoral level.

Professional adult educators perform two basic roles with respect to their responsibilities in the field. On the one hand, they perform an *administrative role* in which they are responsible for the utilization of institutional resources for adult education in keeping with the purposes of the institution. In this capacity they determine program areas, select appropriate methods, manage the operation for the institution, and evaluate the program's effectiveness. On the other hand, professional adult educators may also perform an *instructional role* in which they design and manage the specific instructional activity. In so doing, they are concerned with the sequential ordering of the content, the selection of specific techniques, the management of the learning situation, and the measurement of achievement.

In many instances a single adult educator may perform both roles simultaneously, as is the case with a Home Demonstration Agent who may administrate the program of the Cooperative Extension Service in a county and conduct the various activities herself. This dualism is not unusual; however, the tendency to greater specialization is increasingly separating the two roles. Regardless of which role is performed, the same basic training in adult education is appropriate for both roles.

Education of Adult Educators

Development. The slowly growing recognition and acceptance of adult education as an emerging profession is reflected in the expansion of university curricula for the education of adult educators.

Teachers College, Columbia University, appears to have been the first in the field, with a course on the education of immigrants in 1917. In 1922 it offered the first course which used the term *adult education* in the title. Since that time, an increasing number of institutions have entered or are entering the field to offer graduate work and advanced degrees.

The first doctorate in adult education was conferred by Columbia University in 1935.[3] The University of Chicago followed in 1940. By January 1, 1962, some thirty universities have awarded a doctorate in adult education to 323 individuals. Table 2 lists these universities, the date of the first doctorate awarded, and the total number of degrees conferred to date. Not all the universities listed in Table 2 have graduate programs in adult education; however, they permit students to specialize in the field and to prepare dissertations relating to adult education. Some of the universities—Cornell, for example—have awarded degrees in related fields, such as Cooperative Extension, which fall within the scope of adult education but are not specifically identified as such.

The Commission of the Professors of Adult Education, which is an arm of the Adult Education Association, is composed of representatives from those universities in which a professor is responsible solely for the graduate program in adult education. This Commission is composed of eighteen members representing: Boston University, Brigham Young University, the University of British Columbia, the University of California (at Berkeley and at Los Angeles), the University of Chicago, Columbia University, Florida State University, Indiana University, the University of Michigan, Michigan State University, Ohio State University, and the University of Wisconsin. In each of these institutions students pursue a recognized course of study and complete a dissertation in adult education. As indicated in Table 2, these thirteen universities have awarded 259 of the 323 doctorates in the field. By any standard of measurement, this group forms the hard core of the professionally educated adult educators, although not all of them are still active in the field.

The number of master's degrees earned in adult education certainly exceeds the number of the doctorates, but data on this level are not as detailed. All the thirteen recognized university programs

[3] Cyril O. Houle, "The Doctorate in Adult Education 1961," *Adult Education*, Vol. XII (Spring, 1962), 121–35. See also the same in Spring, 1961, issue.

include graduate study at the master's level and theses related to adult education have been written in many more colleges and universities than those shown in Table 2. With the growth of the field continuing apace, the number of advanced degrees at both levels will continue to increase.

TABLE 2

DOCTORATES IN ADULT EDUCATION, BY INSTITUTION, JANUARY 1, 1962 *

INSTITUTION	YEAR OF FIRST DOCTORATE	TOTAL NUMBER OF DOCTORATES
Columbia University	1935	78
University of Chicago	1940	32
University of Pittsburgh	1942	1
Ohio State University	1945	9
University of California (Los Angeles)	1947	21
University of Illinois	1948	1
University of Michigan	1948	15
Cornell University	1949	32
University of Buffalo	1953	3
Northwestern University	1953	1
University of Wisconsin	1953	66
Indiana University	1954	8
State University of Iowa	1954	2
Stanford University	1955	1
University of Tennessee	1955	1
University of California (Berkeley)	1956	12
University of Denver	1956	2
Florida State University	1956	6
University of Kansas	1956	1
Michigan State University	1956	12
University of Nebraska	1956	1
New York University	1956	8
Texas Technological College	1956	2
Harvard University	1958	1
Iowa State University	1958	1
University of Missouri	1958	1
Syracuse University	1958	2
University of Texas	1959	1
George Washington University	1959	1
Pennsylvania State University	1960	1
Total		323

* Cyril O. Houle, "The Doctorate in Adult Education," *op. cit.*, p. 132. Reprinted by permission of the Adult Education Association.

The basic discipline. Since there is no undergraduate or pre-vocational education in adult education, persons enter the field from some other background usually directly related to the institution in which they perform an adult education function. Thus, adult educators in a library are trained in library service; those in the Cooperative Extension Service are trained in agriculture or in home economics; those in the public schools are usually from the teaching profession; and those in public health are usually nurses, doctors, or sanitarians. The graduate program in adult education, therefore, is built on a wide variety of fields of study that are different but related, so that the essence of the program lies in a core of knowledge pertinent to all these related fields. The graduate student studies adult education in addition to his major field of concentration, sometimes with emphasis on the integration of the two fields.

The universities with recognized graduate programs in adult education have the same basic core courses, although these may vary in title or details.[4] The basic elements of the core are:

1. *A survey course* that introduces the field and discipline of adult education. This will include the history of the development of the field, along with the rationale for adult education. Many students gain their only formal training in the field from this course as it tends to be a service course useful to other fields and disciplines on both an undergraduate and graduate level.[5]
2. *A foundations course* that examines the social, historical, philosophical, and psychological foundations of adult education is usually the first course at the graduate level. It aims to develop an understanding of the importance and function of adult education in modern society as well as the potentialities for continuous learning and the factors and forces that impinge on it.
3. *A program planning course* that examines the learning process and the elements affecting the design of learning situations for adults.
4. *A processes course* in which methods, techniques, and devices are studied in relation to the learning task and the nature of the adults involved.
5. *A community study course* which is concerned with the sociology of the community and the ways in which adult education fits into community institutions. The problem of coordinating educational programs

[4] A detailed report on the development and content of the graduate curriculum is being prepared by the Commission of the Professors of Adult Education.

[5] Watson Dickerman, "A Study of the Introductory Course in Adult Education," *Adult Education,* Vol. X (Autumn, 1959), 50–52.

for adults in a community to insure that social needs are met is an important aspect of community study.

6. *Field work.* Many universities include field work programs which permit students to participate in on-going organizational programs of education for adults. This participation provides opportunities to observe, to apply, and to evaluate the applicability of theory and principles acquired in graduate study.[6]

There are a number of additional specialized courses offered by one university or another that supplement the central core-type courses listed above. Then, too, every graduate student may also draw on any of the resources of his university for such specialized knowledge as may be necessary to round out a program in terms of his objectives.

The content of adult education studies is derived from two basic sources: the social sciences and the humanities, and research in adult education itself. Areas of knowledge borrowed from other disciplines includes substantiated facts and certain appropriate methodology. In every instance, these areas of knowledge are pertinent to the adult education situation; however, they must be interpreted and applied to the solution of the particular problems which face adult educators. The specific knowledge unique to the discipline of adult education relates to the particular problems that arise out of the effort to provide continuing education for adults. The solutions to these problems come from research in adult education, out of which grows theory upon which, in turn, is based further research. Thus, the discipline grows slowly but with logical consistency. Research is presently underway in such areas of interest to adult education as the valid determination of educational needs, the identification of pertinent content, the selection and use of techniques appropriate to both content and learner, the most suitable patterns of organization for education, the measurement of achievement, and the design of a learning situation that fits the needs and abilities of the adult learner.

Characteristics of Adult Educators

The profession. Since adult education is not a clearly perceived professional field, it has no recognized professional group with its

[6] Alan Booth, "A Study of Field Work Programs," *Adult Education,* Vol. XI (Autumn, 1960), 14–18.

own formal organization such as those which characterize older and more stable professions. Those individuals performing adult education functions in the several institutions in society tend to assume membership in professional organizations related to the institution rather than in general associations of adult educators. Thus, library adult educators belong to a professional library association; public health personnel, to a health organization; public school adult educators, to a school-related professional association; and training directors in industry, to their specialized professional society. In most instances, the growth of adult education activities and the increasing numbers of people performing adult education functions have resulted in the formation of special adult education interest groups within the context of existing professional organizations. Thus, we find special adult education interest groups within the American Library Association, the National Education Association, and similar large bodies of professional people. Furthermore, some parts of the adult education enterprise have established specialized associations which operate independently of all other parts. This is illustrated by the National University Extension Association, the Association of University Evening Colleges, the National Association of Public School Adult Educators, or the Society of Training Directors.

This complexity and diversity and the lack of any common perceptions among professional adult educators mirror the diverse nature of the field and make it impossible to identify and study a "typical" adult educator. The nearest approach to this comes through the study of membership in the Adult Education Association (AEA). This organization comes closest to being an unifying association of adult educators and draws its membership from all levels of leadership and every institutional affiliation. Since it has no particular institutional bias and since membership is voluntary, the AEA can be considered to consist of those who identify themselves specifically as adult educators and who have a strong commitment to and interest in the development of adult education generally. AEA members, therefore, are not necessarily representative of all those in adult education. A study of the characterisitics of the AEA membership will describe those who consider themselves to be adult educators.

In 1959, the AEA commissioned the Bureau of Applied Social Research at Columbia University to make a detailed study of its membership. The report of this study provides the best available data about the adult educator as an individual and as a professional person.[7]

Most members of the AEA are persons in paid positions. Only some 14 per cent of the members were reported serving as volunteers; 78 per cent hold paid positions. Of this latter group, 33 per cent were full-time workers in adult education; 58 per cent held a full-time position in another field with some responsibility for adult education; and 8 per cent held a part-time position. This designation of role in adult education is, of course, dependent upon the self-identification by individuals. The fact that they joined AEA in the first place is an indication that they consider themselves to have a specific role as adult educators. The extent and intensity of that role was further specified by the individuals as they designated the degree to which they are involved in adult education.

Those holding paid positions in adult education have done so, on the average, for about ten years. Those holding full-time paid positions in adult education have been in the field the longest. This would seem to indicate that length of tenure and intensity of involvement in adult education influence the individual's self-perception as an adult educator. Those who are newcomers to the field rarely become members of AEA until they have been in the field long enough to begin to feel a sense of identification with it.[8]

This self-identification is illustrated further in Table 3, which shows that those holding full-time paid positions primarily concerned with adult education are most apt to perceive themselves as adult educators; those who perform adult education functions as part of a full-time job in another area have less self-identification as adult educators than those engaged in the field only part-time. These data indicate that as the role in and responsibility for adult education lessens, the individual's perception of himself as an adult educator declines.

---

[7] Edmund deS. Brunner, *et al., The Role of a National Organization in Adult Education* (unpublished report to the Executive Committee of the Adult Education Association, 1959).

[8] William M. Nicholls II and Edmund deS. Brunner, "Composition of AEA's Membership," *Adult Education,* Vol. IX (Summer, 1959), 211–21.

TABLE 3

SELF-DESCRIPTION AS AN "ADULT EDUCATOR" BY THE TYPE OF POSITION HELD IN ADULT EDUCATION
(Expressed in percentages) *

Appropriateness of title of "adult educator"	TYPE OF POSITION IN ADULT EDUCATION					
	All of Full-time Paid	*Part of Full-time Paid*	*Part-time Paid*	*Volunteer or Unpaid*	*No Position*	*Total*
Very appropriate title and often think of self as such	77	40	49	22	14	46
Could appropriately be applied	21	52	41	50	39	42
Not appropriate	2	8	10	28	47	12
	100	100	100	100	100	100

* Edmund deS. Brunner, William L. Nicholls II, and Sam D. Sieber, *The Role of a National Organization in Adult Education* (New York: Bureau of Applied Social Research, Columbia University, 1959), p. 91.

Individuals enter the field of adult education relatively late in their careers. Brunner found the median age to be 35.5 years. Furthermore, 23 per cent did not enter the field until they were forty-two or older, although some 34 per cent of the membership of AEA were employed in the field by the age of thirty-one. Thus, adult education tends to recruit its leadership from other fields at a midpoint in the individual's career rather than gaining its membership directly out of college. This may result from the relative youth of adult education as a line of career development, but it is also affected undoubtedly by the fact that working with adults in an educational capacity requires some experience in being an adult.

Performance levels. In his study of the AEA membership, Brunner, *et al.*, found four major levels of performance within the field: [9]

> "1. Top administrators: Those administering and directing the work of paid adult educators.
>
> 2. Other administrators: Those not directing paid educators but engaged primarily in organizing or justifying adult education programs as well as other leadership activities. . . .

[9] Brunner, *et al., The Role of a National Organization in Adult Education, op. cit.*

3. Broad gauge workers: Those with some of the above administrative activities but also involved in such front line activities as teaching, leading action or discussion groups. . . .

4. Primarily workers: Those with primarily or exclusively front line activities."

The majority of the full-time paid adult educators were classified as top administrators; a majority of the part-time paid and volunteer workers were classified as primarily workers. The details of this analysis of roles is shown in Table 4.

TABLE 4

THE PRIMARY ACTIVITIES CARRIED OUT BY AEA'S MEMBERS BY THE TYPE OF POSITION HELD IN ADULT EDUCATION

(Expressed in percentages) *

Adult Education Activities	*All of Full-time Paid*	*Part of Full-time Paid*	*Part-time Paid*	*Volunteer or Unpaid*	*Total*
Top Administrators	58	31	28	6	35
Other Administrators	15	15	7	6	13
Broad Gauge Workers	13	16	12	12	14
Primarily Workers	11	33	50	65	33
Unclassifiable	3	5	3	11	5
	100	100	100	100	100

* William M. Nicholls II and Edmund de S. Brunner, "Composition of AEA's Membership," *op. cit.*, p. 215.

The variety of institutions involved in adult education complicates the process of identifying the adult educator. Brunner, *et al.*, identified thirteen major types of institutions and agencies with which the members of AEA were affiliated. The universities claimed the largest share (18.7 per cent), followed by the public schools (14.7 per cent), health and welfare (11.9 per cent), and church or religions (10.7 per cent). With respect to full-time paid adult educators, the top three institutions were the universities (27.8 per cent), the public schools (19.8 per cent), and Cooperative Extension (12.9 per cent). Part-time paid adult educators were most numerous in the school system (39.1 per cent) and the universities (26.3 per cent). Those who spend part of a full-time paid position on adult education were predominantly affiliated with health and welfare (16.4 per cent), church organizations (14.2 per cent), and youth organizations (14.1 per cent). Volunteers were found mostly in civic and fraternal organizations (13.5 per cent), health and welfare (12.3 per cent), and church organizations (11.9 per cent). The fewest numbers were found in labor unions, professional associations, governmental agencies, and libraries.

These data indicate that those affiliated with traditional educational institutions are most apt to perceive of themselves as adult educators and to be prompted to join the general organization for adult educators.

Personal characteristics

Sex. Most full-time paid adult educators are male (68 per cent). Among volunteers, however, only 44 per cent are male. Thus, adult education is developing as a career line for men, with women dominating its volunteer aspects.

Age. Brunner, *et al.*, found the median age of adult educators to be 46.4 years, with two-thirds between thirty-five and fifty-four years old. Only 4 per cent are under thirty, which indicates that adult education is not a career line attractive to or holding much promise at present for young people seeking a lifetime professional affiliation. This is further accentuated by the fact that there is no undergraduate or preprofessional training for adult educators; therefore, they enter the field from some other career line later in their professional life.

Education. Adult educators are a highly educated group: 72 per cent have had a graduate education; of this number, 18 per cent, have a doctorate and 54 per cent have a master's degree or its equivalent. Those holding paid positions have more formal education; however, some 52 per cent of those not holding paid positions had a master's degree or its equivalent. This astonishingly high educational level of the self-identified adult educator is influenced by the age at which he enters the field and by the fact that graduate education in adult education usually comes after educational preparation for some other field of endeavor. This does not indicate a high educational requirement for entry into the field but, rather, that the specialized knowledge usually acquired with an advanced degree is recognized and sought by the adult educator.

Residence. Adult educators are predominantly urban residents; some 85 per cent live in a community of 25,000 or over. This is in keeping with the nature of the field, which depends upon a mass clientele for economy, efficiency, and variety of program activities.

Professional organization. Unlike other fields and disciplines, adult education has no single professional organization that provides a visable entity to which all adult educators are attached. Instead, numerous organizations count among their members specialized kinds of adult educators. The major organizations include: [10]

American Association of Museums (museum personnel concerned with the educational as well as the management aspects of museum operations).

American Society of Training Directors (includes those who are primarily concerned with adult education activities conducted under the auspices of business and industry).

Association of University Evening Colleges (those active in the management of evening adult education programs conducted by colleges and universities).

Correctional Education Association (includes personnel involved in the provision of continuing education in penal institutions and establishments).

Great Books Foundation (lay leaders of and participants in study-discussion programs).

National Association of County Agricultural Agents (includes those invloved in agricultural education through the Cooperative Extension Service).

National Association of Public School Adult Educators (administrators, supervisors, principals, and teachers operating public school adult education programs). This organization grew out of the AEA and is now affiliated jointly with the AEA and with the National Education Association.

National Home Demonstration Agents Association (includes those involved in rural adult education through the Cooperative Extension Service).

National University Extension Association (includes personnel in university extension divisions). This is one of the oldest specialized adult education organizations.

Society of Public Health Educators (those concerned primarily with adult education in matters of health who work through the public health system).

In addition to these specialized associations which are composed primarily of adult educators having particular institutional affiliations, there are a variety of professional associations which have subunits or sections concerned with the education of adults. In such

---

[10] See *Handbook of Adult Education in the United States, op. cit.*, Appendix.

units, the emphasis is on the professional concerns of the parent organization as it relates to adult education. Among the organizations in this category are the American Library Association, the American Vocational Association, the American Home Economics Association, the National Recreation Association, the Land Grant Colleges Association, and the National Conference on Social Welfare. In addition, almost every other national association is involved in adult education in one way or another although adult education is not emphasized to any great extent.

The Adult Education Association. There is one general organization of adult educators that draws its membership at random from those engaged in the field. Most of the members of the AEA also hold membership in another related organization and their membership in AEA is to some extent a measure of their commitment to the field of adult education.

The AEA was founded in May, 1951, in an effort to (and with the thus far unfulfilled promise of) creating a strong national organization to unite all adult educators into a single group.[11] That these goals have not yet been achieved is not so much a deprecation of the idea as an indication of the immaturity of the profession. Other parts of the world encounter the same difficulties experienced in the United States and there are many national associations of adult educators in other countries that follow closely the pattern of organization outlined above. In Canada there is the Canadian Association for Adult Education; in England, the National Institute of Adult Education; in Australia, the Australian Association for Adult Education. In every country around the world new organizations are coming into being.

---

[11] Malcolm Knowles, *The Adult Education Movement in the United States* (New York: Holt, Rinehart & Winston, Inc., 1962).

CHAPTER IV

Designing the Learning Experience

At the core of all adult education is the fundamental problem of designing learning experiences that will meet the needs of the participants and achieve the objectives of the sponsoring institution. This is no easy task, and although it is crucial to the success of adult education, it does not often receive the attention from adult educators that it needs. Too many programs are thrown together haphazardly without any clear perception of the purposes for which they are being conducted or of the objectives to be achieved.

The Program Planning Process

Planning educational programs for adults involves certain basic factors that must be given consideration. These include determination of need, identification of educational goals, arrangement of learning tasks, and measurement of achievement. Each of these factors involves various aspects of the adult as a learner, the principles of learning, and the ways in which learning can be facilitated.[1] These are not mutually exclusive categories; each interacts with the others in a variety of ways. The planning process has been and continues to be studied by adult educators but, actually, there is very little known about it or about the interaction of the factors involved. The paucity of valid research makes program planning in adult education still largely a matter of trial and error. Most adult educators operate on the basis of experience largely confined to school educational activities; however, the adult participant exercises the greatest possible influence on the planning through his willingness to participate. This participation tends to temper and refine the school concept into something more appropriate for adults.

Determining needs. Adults are impelled to seek further learning by their awareness of a need for knowledge or skills to solve

[1] See Edmund de S. Brunner *et al., An Overview of Adult Education Research* (Chicago: Adult Education Association, 1959).

problems or to enhance their personal development. This awareness of need motivates them to attend an educational program which they perceive as satisfying their need and conforming to certain expectations. This motive to participate in an educational activity need not necessarily be a motive to learn. Participation in adult education may arise from social needs unrelated to learning, as may be the case with isolated individuals in urban areas who seek to establish some kinds of interpersonal relations and a social group life which they cannot find otherwise. This is a legitimate reason for participation in adult education, but it accentuates the problem of the adult educator in trying to motivate the adult to learn.

When an adult is motivated to learn, he chooses a specific area of content proposed by the adult education program because he anticipates that it will meet his need. In too many instances such unguided selection of a content area may be an unwise choice, resulting from the individual's inability to perceive his need in educational terms. This points up the importance of adequate counseling to insure that the content selected is the right area of study.[2] Correct choice of content, of course, is not the only problem. Since any program cannot be all things to all people, it is necessary to examine with the adult the particular aspects and focus of the content in order that the program will be sure to provide the learning that is needed. In almost every content area, a given group of adults will have varying degrees of previous knowledge and experience that must be taken into account. Thus, the adult educator is concerned not only with the selection and organization of the content to be presented, but also with the characteristics of the participants. No single educational activity can be suited to all classes of participants; therefore, every program requires that the content be selected and arranged for a particular group of participants according to their needs and experiences.

A thorough knowledge of the participants in a program is one of the first steps in the determination of needs. The adult educator should know the age, sex, occupation, previous education, area of residence, stage in the life cycle, political orientation, level of aspiration, level of achievement, attitudes, and a vast array of other social, physiological, and psychological characteristics of his par-

[2] Paul E. Klein, *Counseling Techniques in Adult Education* (New York: McGraw-Hill Book Company, Inc., 1946).

ticipants in order to design learning experiences to meet their needs.

When participants have widely divergent educational backgrounds, they will have different expectations about the program. Those with less educational experience will be more dependent upon the direction provided by an instructional agent in deciding what to learn and how to approach a learning task. They will encounter difficulty in handling new and unfamiliar material, in making relationships between what they know and what they are learning, and in learning to manage the learning process. Those with more educational experience, on the other hand, will be less dependent upon the direction of the instructional agent and, because of their greater familiarity with learning, will be able to achieve greater progress faster. This difference in educational background among participants affects their perception and identification of need and will influence their response to the content and processes introduced by the instructional agent.

The length of educational experience alone is not an adequate measure; the nature and quality of this experience must also be considered. Those with little formal education usually have not internalized democratic procedures applied to the learning situation to the same extent that those with more experience have. Even those with extensive educational experience in highly structured authoritarian situations will encounter the same difficulty. In either case, they will be unable to use democratic procedures effectively and generally; they will be unhappy with any instructional process, such as group discussion, which places the responsibility for learning equally upon the agent and the participant. This avoidance of certain shared responsibilities for the management of the learning situation can be overcome by providing training in the use of the process as a part of the learning task.

Age is another characteristic that influences needs. As individuals advance through the years, their self-perception—and consequently their aspirations—change. In the earlier adult years, the adult male is primarily interested in matters relating to his vocation. He perceives his needs for learning as contributing directly or indirectly to vocational advancement. Women are usually interested in those things directly related to their role of wife and mother. In later years, usually after forty, the adult male begins to recognize that he has probably advanced in his vocation about as far as he can expect to go. With this perception, his needs change from vocational areas to those things that will enhance his personality. He begins to study those subjects that satisfy his nonvocational interests. Women, too, at this period turn toward self-development. With this gradual shift in motivation and needs, an adult's interest in the education process also changes. He is more apt to welcome those processes and procedures that contribute to his enjoyment of the educational task and the other participants.

Research has contributed some knowledge about ways of determining needs. Psychological and sociological research into adult roles and their related developmental tasks provide clues to adult needs in general terms that can be translated into educational programs.[3] Sociological analyses of local community conditions provide ways of identifying social needs.[4] Thus, an analysis of the educational level of the population which shows a very high incidence of functional illiteracy is an indication of the need for fundamental education. If the proportion of a population with less than a high school education is high, then there is a need for high school equivalence programs for adults. Such secondary analysis of data is a valid source for the identification of educational needs in general social terms, but it does not identify the particular individuals who fit the general needs specified. Neither will these procedures detect the special individual educational needs of particular adults.

Many adult educators utilize surveying and polling techniques in an effort to assess individual and community needs and interests in further education. Unless such techniques are used correctly, they can be costly, invalid, and unproductive. The design of surveys and the preparation of research instruments is a highly complex procedure that involves specialized knowledge and skills in order to insure validity, reliability, and objectivity. Without these characteristics, the results can be misleading and may give rise to a misconception of needs and the misdirection of educational programs. Properly

---

[3] Robert J. Havighurst, "Social Roles of the Middle-Aged Person," *Notes and Essays on Education for Adults,* No. 4 (March, 1953). See also Gardner Murphy and Raymond Kuhlen, "Psychological Views of Adult Needs," *Notes and Essays . . .* No. 12 (April, 1955).

[4] Sloan R. Wayland, *et al., Aids to Community Analysis for the School Administrator* (New York: Teachers College, Bureau of Publications, Columbia University, 1956).

managed, surveys and polls can provide highly useful data from which an adult educator can identify needs.[5]

Counseling procedures handled by skilled adult counselors are the best way to uncover personal individual needs. This procedure is obviously costly and limited in scope, since counseling at best can handle but few adults and is not able to assess needs in general community terms.

Many adult educators have found program planning committees composed of interested representatives from the community a very useful and effective way of assessing needs. This procedure is used extensively by the Cooperative Extension Service.[6] Such committee members can extend the range and scope of the adult educator through their extensive contacts in the community. By interviews and discussions with adults throughout the community, they can assess needs and interests with considerable validity. Citizens' committees have added roles in public relations and publicity that help make the program known in the community. By setting adult education goals and objectives for the institution, program planning committees can keep the institution in step with changing community needs and interests. Research indicates that participation in planning by community members tends to result in significantly higher attendance in the programs involved.[7]

Identifying educational goals. The educational goals of a program identify the particular learning tasks to be achieved. They specify the purposes of the program with precision and clarity so that these may be translated into operational terms. Thus, the goal corresponds to a set of observable operations which the participant can be expected to acquire as a result of his involvement in the program. In order to achieve this, the goals must be stated clearly and specifically. This is particularly important since the goals are not only the basis for program design, but also the basis for education.

The clarification of goals may occur on two levels. A long-term

---

[5] Mildred Parten, *Surveys, Polls and Samples* (New York: Harper & Row, Publishers, 1950).

[6] J. L. Matthews, *National Inventory of Extension Methods of Program Determination,* Extension Service Circular 477 (Washington, D.C.: Department of Agriculture, 1952). See also Homer Kempfer, *Identifying Educational Needs of Adults,* Office of Education Circular 330 (Washington, D.C.: USGPO, 1951).

[7] Brunner, *et al., op. cit.,* p. 132.

educational program, such as an evening extension class, a night school course, or a discussion group, involves goals for the total activity and particular goals for each session. The goals for the activity specify the overall purposes of the program, while the particular sessional goals identify the step-by-step achievement needed to achieve the ultimate purpose. Session goals are the components of total program goals. Single-session activities, such as a meeting, have particular goals comparable in definitiveness to session goals and detail the accomplishments expected from the single meeting.

Goals must be stated clearly and simply in order that they can be translated into learning tasks. Expressions such as *increasing understanding* or *developing awareness* are not sufficiently specific to be operational and, therefore, are not functional. What does the word *understanding* mean? Does it mean *knowledge of concepts, changes in attitudes,* or *development of interest?* How can *understanding* be developed through specific learning tasks? What kind of tasks will achieve *understanding?*

When the goals are set, particular topics can be selected that divide the goals into manageable units. These may take the form of questions, issues, or problems. Here, too, care must be exercised. A topic such as "Federal Government Interference in Public Schools" is not a good definition of the topic because the word *interference* prejudges the question of federal participation in education and precludes a valid educational experience involving the gathering and analysis of facts and the application of rational thought to the problem. It would be better to say "An Analysis of Federal Government Participation in Public Education." This is a functional topic that identifies the component learning tasks that can be designed to achieve the goal.

A statement of goal should not be limited to the specific educational program; it should lead to continuous learning after the particular program is concluded. Every part of a program should contain follow-up elements which help the participant relate his learning experiences to his ongoing life in his environment. It should provide motivation for further learning and additional participation in other organized educational activities.[8]

Arrangement of the learning tasks. With the goals set, the next

[8] John McKinley and Robert M. Smith, *Program Planning: A Handbook* (Bloomington, Ind.: Community Services in Adult Education, 1955).

step in the program planning process involves the design of the learning activity. This involves a number of interrelated and interdependent factors that can be identified specifically.

The identification of specific tasks isolates each step in the achievement of the educational goal. These must be arranged in a sequential order: from the known to the unknown, from the simple to the complex, from the participants' state of knowledge to that envisioned in the goal. This is one of the most difficult aspects of program planning and one of the most crucial. It is at this point that the principles of learning play such an important role in planning.

The selection of the appropriate adult educational process is the next step in planning. Processes are selected in terms of the specific nature of the learning task (see p. 86).

The selection of resources, both personal and physical, is another vital factor. The nature and the extent of the content and the learning tasks influence the choice and use of resources. Personnel must be selected on the basis of their competence in the content area, their ability to handle the appropriate instructional process, and their acceptance by the group. Not all experts in a given area of content meet the other two requirements. Familiarity and facility in the use of instructional processes is crucial in the satisfactory diffusion of knowledge, yet this alone does not necessarily insure that an educational experience will be satisfactory to all participants. Acceptability to the group is equally important, although often ignored. The use of a known socialist to manage an instructional experience for a group of men involved in the financial management of a private enterprise is not apt to be conducive to learning. These various aspects of resource selection indicate that resources must be integrated with other aspects of the program.

The measurement of achievement. As stated earlier, the statement of goals identifies the basis for the evaluation of an educational activity. Such evaluation must be built into the program in such a way as to become part of the learning process. This question of evaluation is discussed in more detail elsewhere (see p. 91ff.), but at this point it is necessary to consider it as an aspect of program planning. When evaluation is built into the learning process, it serves both as a check on goal achievement and as a medium for strengthening and extending motivation. Research indicates that awareness of progress is essential to continued learning; therefore, evaluation should provide continuous integrated measurement of progress. Such evaluation must be personal rather than competitive so as to enhance the internal motivation of the participant.

Program Administration

The planning of an educational activity is at the core of adult education; however, as in all social activities, there are certain administrative matters that enter into consideration. Owing to the institutionalization of education, the tendency today is to let administration control rather than facilitate educational planning. The proper role of administration is that of making possible the best educational experience that can be devised to meet the continuing need for learning in modern society. Included in administrative matters are such things as program publicity and promotion, finance, facilities, instructor training and selection, counseling, and scheduling.

Program promotion and publicity. Program promotion involves informing the public of the availability of educational opportunities in such a way as to make them aware of its utility to them and to motivate them to participate and to learn. Adequate and suitable promotion involves selecting the message and media which will reach as many of the potential participants as possible within the limitations imposed by the budget. There are two basic types of promotional situations: the first involves a fairly well identified and limited number of participants; the second involves a large and amorphous audience in which potential participants are not immediately identifiable. Each situation requires different promotional treatment.

When the anticipated participants are known, promotion is not exceptionally difficult. Communication in such situations should be direct. Brochures, personal letters, and similar materials distributed by direct mail will usually suffice. When individuals from this audience share in the program planning process, the interpersonal network of communication is more effective than mass media. The consequences of accepting or rejecting a message are more apparent in a situation of interpersonal communication in which indirect or implied social pressures act to influence decisions. Since participants in the planning process for a particular group are apt to occupy leadership positions in that group, the communication has added impact. These leaders can implement message diffusion more effectively than is possible by other means.

A large unidentified audience presents a different set of communication problems. Mass media are effective here and generally less expensive than direct mail. Since different media have different audiences, the adult educator must select his media in terms of the audience he wishes to contact. If the potential participants in an adult education program are those with an income exceeding $6,000 per year, they are not apt to receive messages diffused through radio stations which aim at an audience composed of wage-earners. Even when free public service announcements are available, they are ineffective if directed at the wrong audience.

Equal in importance to the selection of the media is the timing of the message. Announcements of public affairs seminars, for example, should either immediately precede or immediately follow news broadcasts or news analysis programs since these programs are more apt to attract listeners who are interested in public affairs educational programs. Fine arts program announcements should appear in the theatre or art section of the newspaper, where they are more apt to be seen by those most likely to be interested.

Since different people appear to be primarily oriented to different media, irrespective of their particular educational or social status levels, it is important to know which channels are most effective for which type of adult education program. A study in Louisville, Kentucky, for example, found that newspaper advertisements were more apt than any other media to produce desired responses with respect to shopping practices.[9]

In any communication situation some feedback is an essential part of the communication process. In promoting adult education programs, this feedback may take the form of preregistration inquiries for further information. Newspaper advertisements can include clip-out preregistration forms; radio or television announcements should suggest telephone response. The feedback response should be compatible with the media transmitting the message. Pub-

---

[9] J. L. Matthews and Gale Ueland, *How Consumers Get Information in Louisville,* Extension Service Circular 499 (Washington, D.C.: Department of Agriculture, 1955).

licity used for adult education must inform the potential participant not only of the availability of educational opportunities, but also of their utility and appropriateness for the individual's own interests.

Finance. Adult education is a marginal activity and operates on very limited financial resources. This imposes restrictions on program planning and calls for imaginative thinking as well as careful manipulation on the part of the adult educator. Careful financial management necessitates cost accounting and continuous analysis to insure the most efficient and rewarding use of available funds. Many facets of the adult education program can utilize volunteer assistance from resource personnel and free or inexpensive materials. Although the lack of adequate financial support can inhibit some desirable and creative program activities, it need not be an insurmountable barrier.[10]

Facilities. Education is traditionally equated with schooling, so that facilities for adult education are usually conceived of in terms of classrooms. Such a perception tends to limit and restrict the development of educational activities according to the availability of school facilities. Actually, adult education is the most mobile phase of education. It is adaptable to any situation and is not restricted to the facilities available in any single institution. In many instances, a movement outside the institutional framework is an advantage. The study-discussion programs that have grown popular in recent years emphasize the use of the homes of participants, thus extending adult education into the community.

The use of noninstitutional facilities has the added advantage of carrying the adult education program into the environment in which the adult can feel most at ease. Persons of lower socioeconomic status and limited educational experience are apt to feel uncomfortable in the university setting, whereas they may be induced to participate in educational programs conducted in neighborhood facilities such as churches, community centers, and private homes.

The nature and accessibility of facilities is also related to the age of the anticipated participants. Older adults need facilities suited to their age. Stairs, poor lighting, unsuitable furniture, and an unfriendly environment should be avoided. School furniture designed for pre-adult use, for example, is rarely suited to adult use, and fixed

[10] J. R. Kidd, *Financing Continuing Education* (New York: Scarecrow Press, Inc., 1962).

furniture inhibits the development of rapport and interpersonal relationships so essential to the creation of a suitable learning environment for adults.

Instructor selection and training. The procurement of suitable instructional agents for adult education is one of the most difficult tasks encountered in program planning. The three crucial requirements are mastery of content, competence in an instructional situation, and acceptability to the instructional group. It is rare indeed to find all three qualities in the same person. General practice tends to select agents on the basis of their knowledge of a content area and to assume that the other two ingredients will take care of themselves.

The use of full-time teachers from the day pre-adult program in institutions such as the school or university in evening adult programs offered by those institutions is the normal procedure. This is not necessarily a wise choice, since pre-adult teachers are rarely able to make the adjustments in attitude and instructional style required in adult education.

The in-service training of instructional agents is a useful way of developing understanding and competence in the adult learning situation. This enables a program director to select personnel competent in particular subject-matter areas who can then be trained specifically for their roles as instructional agents. Such a procedure is not generally employed as often as it should be; consequently, many program failures result from the incompetence of the instructors. (This question of leadership and the professional preparation of adult educators is discussed in greater detail on p. 34ff.)

Scheduling. In laying out an institutional program of education for adults, the adult educator must settle major problems dealing with the day, time, and frequency of meetings; the length of session; and the number of sessions for each program. There are no simple rules to guide the decisions respecting these questions, and very little research relating to such problems is available. The accumulated experience of the adult educator in his own community provides the best clues to solving scheduling problems.

Every community has its own accustomed pattern of organization, and the adult educator must study and familiarize himself with the local pattern. In some communities, activities scheduled early in the week evoke a better response than those scheduled later in the week. In other communities, the reverse is true. In general, Monday, Friday, and Saturday nights are not favorable; Wednesday is a bad night in a community strongly oriented toward midweek prayer meetings. Here again, a thorough knowledge of the characteristics of a community is an indispensable prerequisite for program planning.

The normal length of single sessions appears to be two hours. Anything less does not allow enough learning to justify the effort of the participant in attending; anything more tends to induce fatigue that inhibits learning. One session per week is the maximum that an adult will commit himself to attend over a long period of time, as he is usually reluctant to give up more than one evening of his free time in any week. Ten successive meetings appear to be the average duration for an evening activity. A shorter program does not permit the achievement of any fundamental objectives; a longer program would represent a long-term commitment that the adult is reluctant to make. Evening adult classes taken for credit extend through a normal school semester and are dictated by tradition enforced by crediting authorities who are insensitive and indifferent to the requirements of the adult participant. True educational quality is not related to such formalistic elements as time, length of meeting, or duration of program, but rests, rather, in the nature of the learning experience and in the involvement of the participant in a learning task.

Counseling. The provision of counseling service for adults is not normally a part of the adult education program; however, it is tending to become so. Adults need help in analyzing their educational needs and in selecting the particular activity which will be most likely to satisfy those needs. Counseling service should be available regularly for those who wish to make use of it. Adult counseling involves skills different from those normally needed for counseling pre-adults. The adult is less in need of vocational advice and more in need of educational and social guidance. Too many adult problems are unrelated to educational needs, yet many adults look to further education to resolve personal problems that could be resolved better through other means. The ideal adult counselor is one trained both as a clinical psychologist and as an adult educator, so that he can differentiate the needs of an adult and direct him to the proper resource or activity most likely to meet that need.

Selected Program Areas

The adult education enterprise conducts educational programs for adults in almost every subject clustered around every major area of human need for further learning. So vast, so varied, and so diffuse are the opportunities available that it is impossible to provide a complete description or even a cursory examination of the kinds of programs that are offered to adults. At best, this discussion of certain selected program areas will merely illustrate some aspects of adult education.[11]

Academic education. The most traditional program area, which is considered by some to be the only—or at least the most—respectable phase of adult education, is that identifiable as *academic education.* This category includes a program which ". . . involves attainment of credit in a number of courses, is systematic and accumulative, and which leads to a certificate or a degree."[12] Such programs provide adults the same kind of educational experiences available to children and youth. They are largely remedial in the sense that they enable adults to acquire the education which they were not able to acquire for one reason or another earlier in life; therefore, academic education programs for adults provide them an opportunity to remedy the deficiencies of youth. These programs are carried on at three traditional educational levels: elementary, secondary, and university.

Elementary education for adults is an effort to duplicate at an adult level the kinds of learning which prepare the student for the higher forms of academic education. Such programs tend to concentrate primarily upon the tools of learning, such as communication and arithmetical skills. The traditional subject content of elementary school training is not generally appropriate for adults and certainly the time requirements differ.[13]

Secondary education programs for adults are designed for those who have left high school work before achieving a diploma. The high school diploma has become a prerequisite to employment at

[11] For a more complete discussion of the various program areas, see Malcolm S. Knowles (Ed.), *Handbook of Adult Education in the United States* (Chicago: Adult Education Association, 1960), Part IV, pp. 393–550.

[12] Peter E. Siegle, "Academic Education for Adults," *ibid.*, pp. 393.

[13] Angelica Cass, *Adult Elementary Education* (New York: Barnes & Noble, Inc., 1956).

almost any unskilled level; therefore those adults who lack this diploma must acquire it to become employable. The diploma can be achieved in two ways: through the regular high school curriculum offered at times convenient to the adult, or by passing the General Educational Development test. The adult high school curriculum generally copies the regular day program and rarely makes any fundamental concessions to the age, experience, or motivation of the adult. In many instances it requires the same number of class hours per subject as is required in the regular day program. Such inflexible regulations are unrealistic and serve to discourage adults. The General Educational Development program was created in order to accommodate adult experience and to facilitate the successful achievement of the diploma with a minimum of unessential or restrictive regulations. A diploma won by either method is usually acceptable for university entrance.

University education for adults is intended for those who were unable to attend university as undergraduates. These programs are usually offered in the evening through university extension divisions or community junior colleges. In most instances, normal university degree requirements prevail. Since the participants are largely part-time students, it takes them considerably longer to achieve the degree than the usual four years. Some institutions have established special degree or certificate programs designed especially for adults. These special programs give consideration to adult experience in computing degree requirements. New York University has a certificate plan in which an adult must complete forty term hours of university courses and a special project and produce evidence of high school equivalency. He is then permitted to select work of particular interest to himself. The program thereby meets the varying needs and interests of the adult and enables him to choose his own rate of advancement.

The Associate in Arts degree at Syracuse University aims at increasing skills of critical thinking, developing a heightened appreciation of the arts and humanities, and encouraging continued independent study. Harvard University has an Adjunct Arts Degree for which course work can be taken at any cooperating institution in the Boston area. Other institutions, such as Brooklyn College, the University of Oklahoma, and the University of Maryland, have developed special degree programs for adults. The trend in higher adult education is to design programs suited to the characteristics of mature individuals with requirements that are acceptable to the conditions imposed by an active adult life.

Since academic qualification provides a manageable and measurable criterion, and since progressive industrialization demands higher academic qualifications, the growth of special programs for adults will accelerate in the future.[14]

Fundamental education. Fundamental, or literacy, education is the most common form of adult education. At first, literacy education aimed at teaching adults to read and write, but in recent years the concept has broadened to include the minimum education required to operate with competence in modern society. Thus, the designation *fundamental education.* Programs in this area are operated almost exclusively by public school systems with state and (in some instances) federal financial support. They are conducted in both rural and urban areas; however, the rural areas which have the highest illiteracy rates tend to have the fewest programs, owing to the low population density.[15]

Education for later maturity. The slowly rising median age of the population and the rapidly increasing proportion of citizens 65 years of age and over are creating new potential participants in adult education with new and different educational needs. The principal objective of education programs for the older individuals is to help them to develop new goals and activities to sustain them in the later years. Such programs generally break down into two types: programs designed for the elderly themselves, and programs designed for those who work with older adults. There are not many educational programs for the elderly themselves; however, some communities offer special inducements (such as free tuition) to those who wish to enter regular programs. In general, regular adult education programs are not suited to older adults. The physiological and psychological changes that develop with age necessitate special facilities, scheduling, content, and program design in order to serve older adults adequately.

Institutional agents in education, recreation, and health and wel-

---

14 Roger deCrow, *Administrative Practices in University Evening Colleges* (Chicago: Center for the Study of Liberal Education for Adults, 1962).

15 See *Fundamental Education* (Paris: UNESCO, 1949).

fare agencies, among others, need special training for work with older citizens. The familiar materials and processes used with younger adult groups must be adapted to the different needs and characteristics of older adults. Educational programs of this nature are increasing as the recognition of the need grows. These programs usually take the form of short-term workshops, institutes, or conferences. Some universities—notably the University of Michigan, the University of Chicago, and Washington University in St. Louis—have developed graduate programs in this area.[16]

Creative arts. The growth of interest in and programs relating to the creative arts has been extensive in recent years. These programs are directed toward the production, creation, and performance of several art forms; the study and appreciation of art; and the wider distribution of art through traveling exhibits, concerts, and performances. This increasing interest in the arts is manifested in the programs of almost every institution concerned with adult education—notably adult public schools, university extension divisions, the Cooperative Extension Service, and business and industry.

Liberal adult education. Closely related to the creative arts programs are those tenuous activities generally identified as *liberal education.* Although this is a popular category for adult education programs, it is in reality a distinction without a difference and an attempt to attach values and status to particular content areas. Liberal arts programs tend to emphasize the sciences and humanities and to devote particular attention to traditional subject-matter divisions such as anthropology, economics, literature, social science, poetry, music, and similar matters.

Liberal education programs tend to emphasize the discussion group and to use available reading materials under the leadership of nonprofessional discussion leaders. The content does not appear to be related directly to occupational interests or to monetary ends; it is usually interdisciplinary in that any one topic is usually approached through a number of disciplines. Most liberal programs stem from universities, although some public school adult education programs include liberal education courses. Libraries have long

[16] Wilma Donahue, ed. *Education for Later Maturity* (New York: Whiteside Inc., and William Morrow & Co., Inc., 1955).

been active in this field, but not as extensively as have universities. Some private foundations, such as the Great Books Foundation and The Foundation for Continuing Education, are active in this area.[17]

Public affairs education. Programs in various aspects of public affairs are designed to develop knowledge of domestic and international public issues. Implicit in all programs is the stimulation of public interest and the increase of public involvement in decision-making processes. Public affairs programs may be conducted by universities or adult schools under joint sponsorship with voluntary organizations such as the Voice of Women, the League of Women Voters, the American Association for the United Nations, the Foreign Policy Association, and similar groups. These programs may take the form of conferences, short courses, institutes, or residential weekends.[18]

Home and family life education. Programs in this area are conducted by universities, public school systems, churches, voluntary associations, and the Cooperative Extension Service. Such programs are concerned with parent education for child-rearing, homemaking, and intrafamily relationships. This is a large program area in terms of the number of institutions, agencies, and adult participants involved. In 1948, over 42 per cent of the Parent-Teachers Associations conducted parent education programs; in 1957, ninety family welfare agencies provided programs in this area. Nearly every process is used, including discussion groups. In 1959 alone, discussion groups to study the role of parenthood in a free nation were held in 170 communities.[19]

Community development. Although community development is a method of adult education, it is also a program area. This is one of the newly developing areas that is international in scope. It is particularly pertinent to underdeveloped areas, where it is conducted under the auspices of international bodies as well as by national foreign aid programs. The Ford Foundation has been active in a long-term community development program aiding the gov-

---

[17] "Liberal Education," *Notes and Essays,* No. 18 (1957); and Allan B. Knox, *The Audience for Liberal Adult Education* (Chicago: Center for the Study of Liberal Education for Adults, 1962).

[18] Cyril O. Houle and Charles A. Nelson, *The University, The Citizen, and World Affairs* (Washington, D.C.: American Council on Education, 1956).

[19] L. Belle Pollard, *Adult Education for Homemaking,* 2nd ed. (New York: John Wiley & Sons, Inc., 1939).

ernment of India in the development of rural Indian villages. In the United States, various universities have been active in this area for a number of years. One noted program was conducted by the extension department of the University of Virginia.[20] The Universities of Montana, Wisconsin, Michigan, Washington, Southern Illinois, and St. Francis Xavier have been or are now active in this area.

Community development programs usually operate in small towns and in rural areas, but there is an increasing growth of such programs in urban and metropolitan centers. The University of Wisconsin, in particular, has an experimental project dealing with urban community development. These programs, both the urban- and the rural-centered, are concerned with education for community action and emphasize the study and analysis of community needs and resources along with the resolution of these needs. Because they differ so much from traditional programs in adult education, community development programs are often overlooked both as a major program area and as a method of adult education.[21]

---

[20] Jesse Ogden and Jean Ogden, *These Things We Tried* (Charlottesville, Va.: Extension Division, University of Virginia, 1947).

[21] Lowry Nelson, Charles E. Ramsay, and Coolie Verner, *Community Structure and Change* (New York: The Macmillan Company, 1960), pp. 413–42.

CHAPTER V

Managing the Learning Experience

Many people equate education with schooling and, therefore, they are unable to recognize the forms or processes of education that differ from those which traditionally characterize education as it operates in a school setting. Since adult education operates as much outside as within a school situation, there is apt to be more awareness of variety in education here than in any segment of the educational enterprise. Adult education is not bound by any traditional methodological concept, nor does it attach value to any single process beyond its utility in achieving a learning objective efficiently, effectively, and appropriately for the group being educated. Thus, through the study of adult education, it is possible to identify, differentiate, and classify the numerous forms and processes employed to achieve various educational objectives without being hindered by traditional institutionalized conceptions of education.

Three separate elements are included in the notion of processes for adult education, and each of these describes a discrete function. The first element is the *method:* the organization of the prospective participants for purposes of education. The second element involves *techniques:* the variety of ways in which the learning task is managed so as to facilitate learning. The third and final element involves *devices:* all those particular things or conditions which are utilized to augment the techniques and make learning more certain.[1]

Method

The method of education identifies the ways in which people are organized in order to conduct an educational activity. A method establishes a relationship between the learner and the institution or agency through which the educational task is accomplished. Formal

[1] See Coolie Verner, *Adult Education Theory and Method: A Conceptual Scheme for the Identification and Classification of Processes for Adult Education* (Chicago: Adult Education Association, 1962).

educational institutions establish such a relationship for learning by having the participants come to the institution and organizing them into groups according to age, ability, subject matter, or some other criterion. These groups are referred to as *classes*. Since pre-adult education is almost exclusively institutionalized through the school, the principal method employed is the class. Adult education, on the other hand, is not exclusively institutionalized; therefore, it employs the class method as only one in a variety of other methods.

Because method describes a way of organizing participants, the methods of adult education tend to fall into a classification scheme that is predetermined by the ways in which people are naturally organized in the society. People may be found as isolated individuals, as small or large aggregations, or collected into communities. Thus, the methods of adult education can be classified as individual, group, or community methods.

Individual methods. There are many individuals seeking learning who cannot be brought into an institutional setting; therefore, in establishing a relationship with them for purposes of education, the institution must adopt methods that can accommodate isolated individuals. Such isolation of an individual may stem from physical factors—as in the case of those living in rural areas or in isolated outposts, or those who are immobilized by physical disabilities. In some cases the nature of the learning task may be such that the educational activity will be more successful if participants are handled individually rather than in groups. Whatever the causative factors, the design and management of the learning experience is accomplished through the use of methods that serve one individual at a time. Such methods include correspondence study, directed individual study, apprenticeship, and internship. Each of these methods has come into existence in an effort to provide educational opportunities for a particular clientele or to meet a specific instructional problem.

Correspondence study consists of a series of organized lessons or assignments developed sequentially and carried out through an instructor-student relationship that is maintained through the mails. The idea of correspondence instruction originated in 1856, in Berlin. A Frenchman, Charles Toussaint, and a German, Gustav Langenscheidt, joined forces to teach French and German by mail. Each month the students received a printed lesson containing a drill in grammar, exercises in conversation, and installments of a story to translate. Beneath each foreign word in the lesson was a phonetic rendering of the pronunciation and beneath that its translation. This system of language instruction is still used extensively in teaching language by mail.

In the United States, correspondence instruction was started by Dr. William Rainey Harper in 1879 at Chautauqua, New York. In 1890, some time after Harper became president of the new University of Chicago, he instituted the first organized program of university correspondence study. Private correspondence schools trace their origin to Thomas J. Foster, editor of the *Mining Herald* at Shenandoah, Pennsylvania, who started correspondence instruction in 1891.[2]

As a method of instructing adults, correspondence study has many advantages. Students are not excluded from learning by the accident of geographical isolation; they need not be hampered by a regular job or by physical disability; and they can progress at their own rate. It does, however, impose limitations, since not all subject matter is amenable to the restrictions inherent in the method. Furthermore, independent study requires high motivation and intense application which is difficult to maintain, so that the noncompletion rate in correspondence study tends to run higher than the dropout rate in any other method.

Numerous studies comparing the achievement of correspondence students with that of students in regular classes indicate that correspondence students achieve as well or better than resident students, in terms of the factual information acquired. In spite of this, correspondence study tends to be considered inferior and limitations are imposed on the number of correspondence courses that can be applied as credit toward certificates or degrees.[3]

Correspondence study is conducted by university extension departments, by proprietory schools, and by the armed forces. Originally reserved for adults, it is now available at the pre-adult level. Enrollment in all phases of correspondence study tends to be high, but this is offset by the exceedingly low rate of successful comple-

---

[2] John S. Noffsinger, *Correspondence Schools, Lyceums and Chautauquas* (New York: The Macmillan Company, 1926).

[3] Gayle B. Childs, "Research Concerning Supervised Correspondence Study," *National Association of Secondary School Principals,* Bulletin 36 (December, 1952).

tion. Numerous experiments have been made in an effort to raise the rate of successful completion. The Armed Forces Institute has introduced supervised group study on military bases and universities are encouraging instructor-student personal contacts. In spite of the negative aspects of correspondence study, it constitutes one of the major methods in adult education.

Apprenticeship and internship are individual methods employed when the nature of the learning task is such that skills and knowledge can be acquired best through practice under instructional supervision. These methods are used extensively in vocational areas and in certain professions. They constitute the earliest forms of education, and although they have never been fully replaced by later methods, it is only recently that they have been employed systematically by educational institutions.

Directed individual study is the method preferred for adult education by some institutions, such as the library. The Readers' Advisor in a library operates on the basis of individual contacts by helping individuals find the material needed to pursue their private studies.[4] In many respects, this method is a form of adult counseling with an instructional rather than therapeutic orientation.

Group methods. Group methods for adult education involve a number of individuals in the educational activity simultaneously. These methods may be employed by the institution in establishing relationships for learning with existing groups or in forming groups for instruction. Existing groups may include the family, or autonomous groups, or social organizations such as formal associations. In forming instructional groups, otherwise isolated individuals are collected for efficiency or expediency and a direct relationship for learning is established among the participants and between them and the instructional agent. The learning achieved in groups may be essentially individual learning, or it may be group learning, depending on the psychic nature of the group. Size appears to be a major influence on the nature of the learning accomplished. The larger the group, the more apt it is to achieve individual rather than group learning, because numbers appear to influence the interrelationships among group members. Certain kinds of learning objectives can be achieved successfully in large groups while other

[4] Jennie M. Flexner and Byron C. Hopkins, *Readers' Advisors at Work* (New York: American Association for Adult Education, 1941).

objectives can be accomplished only in smaller, more intimate groups. If the learning objective is confined to the acquisition of facts or information, the size of the group is unimportant; but where the objectives include alterations in social behavior patterns and attitudes, the smaller group is more effective because member interaction supplements the instructional procedures. Certain group methods require that the size of the group be limited but, in general, the method is not influenced by size although the nature of the learning objectives achieved is.

The class is the most familiar group method as it is used traditionally by formal educational institutions. It is a group pattern in which isolated individuals are gathered together, for purposes of efficiency and economy, into an instructional group. A class is "a sequence of learning experiences arranged in a systematic order of predetermined duration generally structured around a limited segment of knowledge in which the agent is charged specifically with the general direction, organization, and control of the learning experience."[5] There are many variations in the class, but these in no way alter its fundamental nature. In England, the *tutorial class* represents a highly respected version. In this form the class is of three years' duration. The *sessional class* is more popular in this country and is gradually replacing the tutorial class in England. The class method dominates adult public night school programs and university evening extension programs.

Although a class is basically a collection of individuals, it may, under certain circumstances, become a unit in which the social processes of the group exert a major influence on learning. The differentiation depends upon the skill and management of the instructional agent and the nature of the learning objective. The class method tends to dominate educational methodology and to be employed regardless of whether or not it is the best method to use in terms of the nature of the participants and the educational objective. The use of a variety of techniques within the class structure can extend its utility; however, the lecture and the question-and-answer techniques remain the most common devices.

Discussion groups are a newer concept in instructional methodology that have assumed the position of a panacea. A discussion group

---

[5] Verner, *op. cit.*, p. 5.

provides "a learning situation which conforms to the characteristics and societal processes of a group so that learning is achieved in the group as a unit as well as by the individual members. The responsibility for learning is shared by the group members and the agent." [6]

The discussion group differs materially from the class. In the discussion group, the content is determined and controlled by the participants rather than by the instructional agent alone and its organization results from group interests and progress. Although discussion is a major technique, the discussion group may frequently use the lecture, role-playing, and panel discussion, as well as a variety of devices. Discussion groups are promoted avidly by a number of foundations, such as The Great Books Foundation or The Foundation for Continuing Education. It is used extensively by university extension divisions and libraries, but rarely by public evening adult schools. In some instances, the class is used under the pretext that it is a discussion group. One major advantage of the discussion group in terms of the organization of people for learning is the fact that, since such groups must normally be limited to something like twelve participants, they can convene in any convenient place and need not be restricted to institutional facilities. This noninstitutional pattern is characteristic of many discussion group programs and they are sometimes referred to as "livingroom learning" because they can meet conveniently in members' homes.

Comparative research studies show that the discussion group is equal or superior to other methods when the educational objective involves alterations in socially based behavior, attitude changes, or group decision-making. It is effective for developing depth in understanding concepts, for recognizing relationships, and for integrating learning with experience. It is not useful in teaching manipulative skills or content acquisition. Discussion is a sophisticated method requiring a particular kind of participant. Studies of characteristics of participants in various methods show that those in discussion groups differ from others by having a higher educational level, higher socioeconomic status, and higher social participation scores. Furthermore, successful discussion groups tend to attract those with more rather than less experience in educational activities. The choice of group discussion, therefore, is influenced by the objectives

---

[6] *Ibid.*, p. 6.

of the educational activity, the nature of the learning task, and the previous experience, sophistication, and sociocultural characteristics of the learners.[7]

The *workshop,* or *institute,* is another of the newer methods popular with adult educators. This consists of a learning situation in which the activity is concentrated in a limited period of time, as, for instance, two or three successive days. It usually has some of the characteristics of a class and of a discussion group with a variety of techniques in evidence. Workshops are frequently residential.[8]

The *meeting* vies with the class in popularity, particularly among the less formal institutionalized programs of adult education. The meeting is generally a single instructional session, although it may be composed of a series of single or related sessions. It is used extensively in library-sponsored adult education and by the Cooperative Extension Service. Meetings are particularly useful for conveying information, but rarely effective for teaching complex and involved learning tasks. The use of the meeting as an educational method is sometimes confused or combined with the use of the meeting as an organizational or associational pattern of operation. Research indicates that the meeting increases in effectiveness as the educational level of participants rises. Thus, those with higher educational levels are more apt to attend meetings and to learn than are those with lower educational levels. The effectiveness of the meeting in achieving educational objectives is directly associated with the care given to the planning. In many respects the meeting has characteristics similar to the class, and the lecture or speech tends to be the more usual technique employed in them.[9]

The *forum,* or *assembly,* is a common method employed for large groups. In many respects this method is indistinguishable from the meeting; however, it is used when larger groups are involved and when the learning objective is confined to the diffusion of information or opinion. Forums tend to use the lecture or panel techniques along with such illustrative devices as films or slides. There are many variations on the forum, such as a film-forum, a lecture series,

---

[7] Edmund de S. Brunner, *et al., An Overview of Adult Education Research* (Chicago: Adult Education Association, 1959).

[8] Earl J. Kelley, *The Workshop Way of Learning* (New York: Harper & Row, Publishers, 1951).

[9] Lucinda Crile, *Findings from Research on Meetings* (Washington, D.C.: U.S. Department of Agriculture, 1956).

or a panel forum. The forum has very limited audience participation, although participation may be increased through the use of the Phillips 66 discussion technique or adaptations of it.

Community methods. The community provides a setting in which the common problems encountered in living become the basis for the educational activity. This alliance creates an educational method in which study and action are virtually indistinguishable. The primary community method is community development. This is often not identified as an educational method because of its integration of study and action; however, there is a distinction between the two and adult education is concerned only with study that may lead to action.

Techniques

The techniques of adult education identify the ways in which the instructional agent establishes a relationship between the learner and the learning task. The utility of a given technique depends on its appropriateness for the particular learning task. Techniques are classified in terms of the kinds of learning tasks for which each is most useful.[10]

To acquire information. The search for information and knowledge is one of the major motivating forces that prompt people to participate in adult education; therefore, those techniques which provide facts or data with the greatest facility and least effort on the part of the learner are preferred by most adults. Thus, information-giving techniques are used more extensively than any others. They are particularly suited to large groups and are used in meetings, forums, and workshops.

The *lecture,* or *speech,* is the most familiar and most widely used of the information-giving techniques. A lecture is a discourse on a particular subject organized logically so as to present the maximum information with a minimum of complexity. The lecture is among the oldest educational techniques; it came into being because the scholars who had the information were the only source of it. Now that printing and other media of mass communication have facilitated access to desired information, there is no longer a need for

[10] Verner, *op. cit.*, pp. 19–23.

TABLE 5

INFORMATION TYPE TECHNIQUE *

Technique	*Size of Group* **	*Situation in Which Employed*
Lecture	Any size	When an expert is required to inform a highly interested and fairly knowledgeable group.
Lecture with devices Records Tape TV Film Skits Charts, maps, etc. Radio	Any size	When an expert is requested to inform and (a) the content lends itself to illustration by means of such devices, or (b) the group is not well informed on the subject.
Speech	Any size	When the purpose is to present a particular point of view to a group where the agent has used speech preparation as a device to cause the speaker to study a specific area intensely and also to inform the group through his findings.
Debate	Medium to large	When there are conflicting views on a subject which could be elucidated by a statement of each by an expert and clarified further by argument between them.
Symposium	Medium to large	When different authoritative opinions on a subject of some interest to the group are to be presented.
Dialogue	Medium to large	When different views on an issue are to be presented where none is presented as the final solution but where the dialogue aims at revealing all aspects of the problem and perhaps at compromise.
Panel	Medium to large	When a number of views, attitudes and evaluations on a given subject are to be presented, where none is yet seen as the final solution. The thinking of members of the panel on the issue under consideration may develop during the course of the panel.

Lecture-forum Lecture with devices-forum Speech-forum Debate-forum Symposium-forum Dialogue-forum Panel-forum	Same as for technique without forum	When audience participation has been built into the learning situation and the aim is to provide members of the audience with an opportunity to integrate the information with their own thinking and experience.
Field trips	Small and medium	When the object is to give knowledge of how a process is accomplished in the actual situation.
Study guide	Individual	When the learner cannot come into direct contact with the agent, the study guide provides an outline whereby the learner may gain knowledge in a systematic way. Forum-type benefits can be insured by notes back and forth between agent and student.

* Constructed by Margaret Stott.
** Group sizes are designated as follows: small (less than 20); medium (20 to 50); large (over 50).

scholars to lecture in order to diffuse information. In view of this, the function and purpose of the lecture have changed. At present, its primary purpose is to set a common frame of reference for learning.

Research studies indicate that shorter, well-prepared lectures are better than longer lectures (thirty minutes appear to be the optimum length). When compared with group discussion, the lecture appears to be better for immediate recall but less effective for delayed recall. Lectures alone seem to bring about little change in behavior and are not as effective for learning as when they are combined with other techniques, such as discussion or demonstration. Since most adults are preconditioned to the lecture, it is generally effective with any group.

The *panel* is a popular modification of the lecture. It operates either as a series of small lectures by panel members or as orderly, well-organized conversation by a group with specialized knowledge of the topic under discussion. Like the lecture, the panel provides little opportunity for participation by the learner unless it is used in conjunction with other techniques.

These and other information-giving techniques are of limited utility, yet they are used more extensively than other adult education techniques. Too often, they are selected without reference to the fundamental objectives of the learning situation. They require the least involvement of the participant; therefore, the responsibility for the success of the venture lies almost wholly with the instructional agent. In some respects they are the easiest techniques to use and with certain groups they may prove to be the most effective. Immature individuals, or those with little experience in assuming responsibility for their own learning, find the information-giving techniques most satisfactory.[11] Some common techniques in this classification are listed in Table 5.

To acquire a skill. Skill-learning—whether cognitive, verbal, or manipulative—requires different educational management than does the acquisition of information. Among other things, the learner must assume a more active role in the learning process; therefore, the techniques in this category must be those that provide greater opportunities for participation (see Table 6).

---

[11] Brunner, *et al., op. cit.,* p. 168.

The *process demonstration* is a useful technique for instructing in manipulative operations that must be acquired in order to develop skill and proficiency in performing specific tasks. It can also be used in certain tasks involving the learning of some verbal and cognitive skills. In the process demonstration, the component steps in the performance of a selected task are isolated and taught in sequential order. Mastery of each step is a prerequisite to proceeding to the next step. The technique is used by the instructional agent to show the operations involved in the task, and these are then reproduced by the learner to reinforce the learning.

Role-playing is a relatively new technique useful in certain kinds of verbal and cognitive skill-learning. By assuming or acting out a "role," the learner has an opportunity to understand the attitudes, perspective, and behavior of the individual whose role he is playing. In order for the technique to be useful, the issue being acted out must evoke strong feelings in the participants. The technique has been found to be ineffective when the participants are neutral about the subject. It is not a good technique to use with rigid personalities nor will it change those who hold strongly to opinions or who have fixed attitudes. Brunner notes ". . . that the technique of role-playing should not be uncritically accepted by adult educators. Research is needed to determine what sort of people, kinds of topics, purposes and situations lend themselves to its effective use, and to determine more precisely just what are the significant or effective factors in the role-playing." [12]

Drill, or *practice,* is a technique that is particularly useful in reinforcing learning. It enables the learner to repeat, at his own speed, step-by-step procedures involved in a given learning task. Thus, variable rates of learning ability can be accommodated. In learning manipulative skills, more instructional time must be devoted to practice than to anything else. In the initial stages of learning, practice sessions should receive close instructional supervision to insure that incorrect responses are corrected before they become set. Once correct responses are learned, the learner can then proceed to drill himself. Teaching machines are particularly effective devices for use with drill in certain situations.

[12] *Ibid.,* p. 147. See also Alan Klein, *Role-Playing* (New York: Association Press, 1956).

TABLE 6

APPLICATION-TYPE TECHNIQUES *

Technique	*Size of Group* **	*Situation in Which Employed*
Buzz groups	Any size, about 200 maximum	When the lecturer wishes to "sound out" the interests of his audience in his subject, he can assign buzz groups to formulate questions. The agent can also use them when he wishes a large or medium group to have an opportunity to relate different aspects of the content to their own thinking and experience.
Group discussion	Small	To gain greater participation by the members in the learning task in order that they may work out the relationship of the material under discussion to problems which concern them.
Round table	Small	For the intensive analysis of a specific problem common to the experience of all those present and usually with a solution as the desired end.
Seminar	Small	To direct a group of advanced students in their projects, giving them an opportunity to learn through discussing their projects with others.
Colloquium	Small	With an advanced group in which research projects are planned and evaluated as they progress.
Colloquy	Small	To combine expert knowledge with high audience participation in order to achieve high correlation of expert knowledge with problems which the group has gathered to solve.
Role-playing	Small	To enable the participants to enter more fully into the ideas, thoughts, and feelings brought out in the topic under consideration.
Sociodrama	Small	Sociodrama is role-playing dealing specifically with problems of a social nature determined and constructed by the group itself. It is used in situations where greater comprehension of social problems is desirable.
Case study	Small	To help participants see the application of previously learned principles and knowledge to a specific case and thereby to help them gain some understanding of the application of principle to practice.

Setting up and carrying out projects under supervision (still educationally)	Small	To provide an opportunity for previously learned principles and knowledge to be thought through in their application to a specific project which is then carried out in an educationally controlled way so that learning may be continuous throughout the experiment.
Field work under supervision (performance in real life situations)	Individual or small	Participant works in a practical situation while endeavoring to relate previously learned principles and knowledge. The agent appoints a person who is more highly trained from this same practical milieu to aid the student in his perceptions.
Process-demonstration	Any size	When the agent verbally explains and demonstrates, or has demonstrated, the process step by step in order that the group can understand the process before trying to reproduce it.
Practice	Individuals, small and medium groups	When the individual or group performs the activity subject to correction by the agent.
Drill or overlearning	Individuals, small or medium groups	When the purpose is to create an automatic response, the agent causes the group to practice the activity past the point needed for recall.
Simulated performance or dry run	Small or medium groups	Used to provide experience in a situation as near to the real as possible where the use of the real situation might injure the learner, the equipment or both (as in war games, learning to fly a plane, and so on.) A series of separately learned tasks are combined in this situation.
Listening teams	Any size	When it is desired to develop critical listening skills and to concentrate attention of the subject at hand.

* Constructed by Margaret Stott.
** Group sizes are designated as follows: small (less than 20); medium (20 to 50); large (over 50).

There are many other techniques that are useful in skill-learning; however, more than one is usually required in any complete skill instructional situation. There are three basic phases in skill-learning and each requires different techniques.

1. *Building a concept of the skill.* This is usually achieved through explanation (i.e., lecture), demonstration, and study (i.e., reading manuals, instructional sheets, and the like).
2. *Developing the skill.* This is usually done through performance of the steps or stages in the task (under direction of the instructional agent), followed by supervised practice to correct performance and reinforce learning. This can be done individually or in groups.
3. *Continuing practice.* This is necessary to develop accuracy and speed in performing the task to the point where it becomes almost an automatic procedure. At this point, the learner should have sufficient competence to proceed on his own at his own rate of development. Continuous evaluation of performance is essential to insure reinforcement.

To apply knowledge. Most adults seek further learning to satisfy some pressing personal need. Information alone is not enough; it is also necessary to learn how to apply informaton to the solution of a problem. This requires the integration of knowledge and the use of intellectual processes. Since this is a different kind of learning task from either the acquisition of information or the development of skills, it necessitates the use of techniques which encourage thinking, evaluation, and trial; therefore, these techniques must provide for a very high degree of involvement on the part of the learner. The problem-solving process involves several steps: (1) identification of the problem; (2) collection of needed information; (3) selection of trial solutions; (4) evaluation of possible solutions; and (5) choice of the best solution. Any techniques employed must emphasize this problem-solving process rather than an approved solution. Shared participation in the learning task is necessary in order that the process can be evaluated (see Table 6).

Group discussion is one of the best techniques for problem-solving, for it provides techniques for problem-solving as it provides opportunity for extensive participation in the process of helping a group identify, examine, and solve a problem. "Discussion implies a face-to-face interacting group of persons engaged in a directed conversation about a topic of mutual interest in which they share both information and opinoins or raise questions with respect to the subject under consideration." [13]

Numerous research studies have compared the effectiveness of discussion with that of other techniques, such as the lecture. Although the results of research are not conclusive, it would appear that discussion is definitely preferred in situations where the learning objective involves group behavioral or attitudinal change. Furthermore, when group decisions are involved, more "good" decisions arise out of discussion than from the use of any other technique. In terms of the quantitative learning of measurable facts, the lecture is superior to discussion with respect to immediate recall, but discussion is superior in delayed recall.

In many circles the term *group discussion* is too loosely applied to any exchange between the instructional agent and the learner, such as that which occurs in a question-and-answer situation. True discussion is differentiated from other exchanges among group members by the role and status of the instructional agent. Although good discussion leadership is essential, the leader must also be acceptable to the group in the same status relationship as all members have to each other. This differs appreciably from the authority position which identifies the instructional agent in the use of other techniques. Although discussion is not always the appropriate technique for every specific learning task, there are other values derived from its use which are not associated with the content under discussion. There are many subsidiary social values derived from the interaction characteristic of group discussion; however, these are not usually the instructional objectives of an activity and do not, of themselves, justify the assumption that group discussion is an end in itself.

The *buzz group* or *Phillip's 66 discussion* is a modification of group discussion that has specific utility in certain learning situations. This technique uses small groups of six to ten members to discuss a single specific item for a brief period (from six to ten minutes). It is particularly useful as a means of providing for or increasing learner participation in a meeting or in a large class. When used in conjunction with a lecture, for example, it can insure and control questions raised by the audience. With a panel, the buzz group can

[13] *Ibid.,* p. 164.

be used to express the audience's specific interests in a topic to insure that the panel discusses the topic within the audience's frame of reference. Since the buzz group need not involve the movement of the audience, it is well suited to large groups of any size. Its effectiveness is limited to a single, well-defined task and it should not be used as a substitute for group discussion for it is basically a leaderless group.

These and many other techniques in adult education are subject to infinite variation through mutations, amalgamations, and modifications. The range of potentially useful techniques is limited only by the creative imagination of the instructional agent who must devise ways of helping the learner achieve his educational goal.

Devices

The term *devices* is a convenient way of identifying the many instructional aids that extend or increase the effectiveness of methods and techniques but which cannot themselves instruct. Items in this category range from instructional materials to communication media and from illustrations to the arrangement of furniture. Like the other processes, they have variable efficiency in different instructional settings for a number of purposes. Because of their utility in many situations, some devices may be erroneously identified as methods or techniques although they cannot perform the same functions. Devices are classified in terms of their inherent nature and the function they perform in the instructional setting.

Illustrative devices. Nearly every learning task is strengthened by the use of illustrations of one kind or another. These may include a verbal illustration, such as a lecture; or visual illustrations, such as still pictures or slides; audiovisual illustrations, such as motion pictures; or result demonstrations. There is such a variety of devices in this category that only a minute selection can be discussed here.

The *result demonstration* is used extensively in agriculture and in armed forces education. This device is effective in showing the result to be achieved through the application of information and skill. A field of corn or wheat will demonstrate the value of a particular fertilizer or of a special plowing and planting procedure. A finished garment, a machined part, a typed page, or a plate of pastries can be used to show the result of a well-handled manipulative skill.[14]

Films and similar audiovisual devices are used extensively in a variety of ways in adult education. They can be particularly effective in illustrating a subject, in showing interpersonal relationships, in demonstrating a process or steps in a skill, and in providing information. The Film-Forum is an illustration of the use of a single device which replaces the lecturer for specific instructional purposes. Research indicates that films are effective media for conveying information, but that the learning achieved through films is closely related to the educational level of the participant. Films achieve their maximum effectiveness when they are used as adjuncts to a technique; therefore, they should not be the sole educational process employed.[15]

Extension devices. These devices extend the reach of an educational method to individuals beyond the range normally expected in an institutional setting. *Radio* and *television* are used for this purpose. Early studies of radio broadcasts showed that radio was an effective device for learning and that the measurable content acquired through radio differed little, in terms of immediate or delayed recall, from that acquired alone. Like with the lecture, however, it is more effective when combined with a technique like discussion. This use of radio and group discussion is illustrated by the Canadian Farm Radio Forum: listening groups across Canada discussed the material presented by the radio forum and then communicated by mail with program personnel.[16]

Television is being used with increasing frequency as a means of extending the reach of a method to large audiences. Television has some obvious advantages over radio since it combines sight and sound. It has been found to be more effective than radio for a great variety of educational tasks, including the learning of a skill such as dressmaking. The effective use of both radio and television is increased by the establishment of some sort of two-way communication between the agent and the learner. Even the most minimal contact is valuable and a combination of radio or television with

14 *Result Demonstration Manual,* Handbook 123 (Washington, D. C.: U.S. Department of Agriculture, January, 1957).

15 Brunner, *et al., op. cit.*

16 R. Alex Sim, *Canada's Farm Radio Forum* (Paris: UNESCO, 1954).

correspondence study appears to increase the effectiveness of that method.

Environmental devices. There has been little study of the influence of environmental conditions on learning. In one instance, the way in which seating is arranged has been found to influence the productivity of a discussion group. Attempts to conduct discussion in rooms with seats arranged in rigid rows have not been successful. Movable seats that can be arranged in a circle or around a table are essential to successful discussion. The buzz group represents a technique designed to overcome the problems encountered with fixed seating.

Manipulative devices. Training in manipulative skills depends heavily upon the availability of manipulative devices. Included in this category would be the vast range of equipment involved in the skill being learned, since the proper use of tools and equipment is an essential part of the mastery of any skill. Working models come into this category because they illustrate the function and relationship of component parts in motion. There has been some research by the military services and in vocational education into the effective use of manipulative devices which has proven the utility of these devices when employed correctly at the appropriate stage in the learning activity. More detailed and specific research is needed, however, with respect to all classes of devices.

Selection of Processes

In the design and management of adult education programs, the most crucial task facing the adult educator is the selection of the right process. A competent choice requires extensive knowledge of the learning process, of the nature and interaction of groups, of the sociocultural characteristics of participants, and of the efficacy and appropriateness of the various methods, techniques, and devices.

Since method is a matter of organization for learning, the selection of method is determined by a combination of factors:

1. The possible ways in which the potential learners might be organized;
2. The nature and objectives of the specific learning program;
3. The resources and capabilities of the institution or agency offering the program.

In some instances these elements may come into conflict so that no educational program can be conducted for a particular group. A particular group may be so situated geographically that an individual method is required, but the nature of the learning objective may be such that it can only be achieved through a small-group method. On the other hand, the participants and the objectives may lend themselves to individual methods but the institution may not be equipped to handle anything beyond the class method. When all the factors are considered, it is usually necessary to arrive at a compromise choice that may eliminate some potential participants or exclude some of the desired learning objectives. In general, institutions concerned with the education of adults tend to operate within the framework of a particular group of methods and the selection of method is not a matter of completely free choice.

The selection of techniques and devices is the responsibility of the instructional agent. In this case many different but interdependent factors come into play which must be reconciled in order to arrive at the appropriate technique.

Conditions imposed by the method. Since method determines the organization of the educational program, it imposes limitations on the techniques and devices which can be used. Individual methods—such as correspondence, for example—preclude the use of any techniques involving face-to-face interaction among learners; therefore, group discussion cannot be used. Not all methods impose such obvious limitations, but each method tends to restrict the range of choice respecting the use of techniques and devices.

Nature of the learning task. Some learning objectives and their component learning tasks predetermine the range and variety of appropriate techniques. Objectives and tasks within the area of manipulative skills cannot be accomplished effectively through the use of information-type techniques. Although it may be possible to teach a person to drive a car through the use of the lecture technique, this is not efficient nor is it likely to achieve the same level of skill proficiency that could be reached through the use of more appropriate techniques. Although there is too little definitive research to allow any prescription of techniques to tasks, such research as has been done indicates that any learning objective is achieved more successfully when a variety of techniques and devices is employed. Thus, a lecture may be appropriate for some of the specific tasks associated with a skill objective but the maximum achievement of skill will depend upon the use of the lecture in conjunction with a variety of other things such as demonstration, supervised practice, drill, and films or working models. No single technique is adequate for any single objective; therefore, a variety of techniques must be selected to fit the various component tasks which lead to the objective.

Characteristics and experience of the participants. Individuals bring to each learning task a wide range of knowledge, experience, and attitudes which influence their responses. These factors can facilitate or inhibit the effective use of a given technique in a particular situation. Very few individuals, for example, are equipped to handle their personal responsibilities as productive group members in a group discussion because most people have a generally low level of previous experience with discussion. Lack of experience may affect the learner's attitude toward discussion as an appropriate instructional technique. Furthermore, the demand for "practical" learning in the shortest possible time will cause participants to resist techniques that they may consider to be time-wasting. In general, the lower the educational level of the learner, the more apt he is to rely on information-type techniques and the less he wants to participate in the learning process.

The number of participants involved in any single activity affects the selection and use of techniques. Group discussion cannot be used effectively in a large group meeting managed by a single instructional agent, nor, conversely, is a panel the most efficient technique for a small discussion group.

Abilities of the instructional agent. The demand for adult education is so great and the supply of adult educators so small that many people are utilized as instructional agents who are unfamiliar with the learning process and with the variety and suitability of techniques and devices. Such agents tend to manage the learning situation intuitively by selecting and using the instructional techniques with which they are familiar.

Inherent efficiency of the technique. Techniques are devised to achieve particular kinds of learning objectives and have, therefore, certain inherent limitations that determine the situations in which they are effective. These limitations are closely related to the nature of the learning task and the restrictions which it imposes.

Some techniques are abstract and, therefore, cannot be used appropriately in situations involving concrete learning. Information-type techniques are inherently abstract and not appropriate for the kind of applied learning that is required for manipulative skills or for problem-solving. Some techniques provide for a minimal involvement of the learner in the learning task and are not suited to use in situations where a high measure of learner participation is required. There is virtually no research in this area to provide a guide to selection in terms of the inherent qualities of a technique.

Availability of facilities and equipment. An educational setting is rarely ideally suited to the particular activity for which it is used. Adult education is particularly inhibited by inadequate facilities and equipment, since it usually goes on in places designed for other groups and other activities. This condition does impose some limitations on the management of the learning activity and may prevent the use of particular techniques or devices that are especially desirable. Adult educators have long since learned to "make do" by operating as effectively as possible within the limitations imposed by their environment.

Nature of the learning process. The learning process itself imposes certain requirements on the instructional situation that must be considered. These requirements in adult education are different from those characteristic of pre-adult learning, but the difference is a matter of emphasis rather than of kind. There is no argument any longer about adult abilities with respect to learning, but there is need for further research to clarify some of the unanswered questions about the management of learning situations for adults. Some of the principles of learning particularly relevant to adult education can be summarized as follows: [17]

(a) Learning is an active process and adults prefer to participate actively; therefore, those techniques which make provisions for active participation will achieve more learning faster than those that do not.

(b) Group learning is more effective than individual learning; therefore, those techniques based on group participation are more effective than those which handle individuals as isolated units.

(c) Learning that is applied immediately is retained longer and is more subject to immediate use than that which is not; therefore, tech-

---

[17] Brunner, *et al., op. cit.,* Chap. 2.

niques must be employed that encourage the immediate application of new material in a practical way.

(d) Learning must be reinforced; therefore, techniques must be used that insure reinforcement.

(e) Learning new material is facilitated when it is related to what is already known; therefore, the techniques used should help the adult establish this relationship and integration of material.

(f) The existence of periodic plateaus in the rate of learning necessitates frequent changes in the nature of the learning task to insure continuous progress; therefore, techniques should be changed frequently in any given session.

(g) Learning is facilitated when the learner is aware of his progress; therefore, techniques should be used that provide opportunities for self-appraisal.

The design and management of a learning situation is enhanced when planning for learning takes into account an analysis of the particular techniques appropriate to each task, and an understanding of the characteristics of the learner in the social situation established for learning. The more careful the planning, the more the learning that will be achieved.

CHAPTER VI

Evaluating the Activity

Evaluation identifies the process used in determining how well an educational activity is producing the objectives set for it. "The primary purpose of evaluation in education is to find out how much growth and change have taken place as a result of educational experiences." [1] Evaluation as such has not seriously concerned adult educators in the past, for, as Essert notes:

> To a major extent adult education stands on its own merits. . . . In the final analysis there is no need for elaborate schemes of evaluation.[2]

This earlier disinterest in evaluation stemmed partly from the nature of adult education itself and partly, from the absence of any suitable conceptual framework or adequate instruments for meaningful evaluation. This situation is changing rapidly with the development of the discipline of adult education and with the increase in systematic research related to problems of interest and concern to the field. There has always been some kind of assessment and measurement, but it has not been systematic, scientifically accurate, or particularly useful to adult educators.

Why Evaluate

Evaluation is important to every human endeavor as a means of measuring progress or achievement. It is particularly important as a way of determining the worth of adult education to society and appraising the efficiency and effectiveness of the ways it performs the tasks society has set for it. In crass terms, evaluation can determine whether or not the time, energy, and money expended in planning

---

[1] Committee on Evaluation, *Program Evaluation in Adult Education* (Chicago: Adult Education Association, 1952), p. 3.

[2] Paul L. Essert, *Creative Leadership of Adult Education* (Englewood Cliffs, N. J.: Prentice-Hall, Inc., 1951), p. 161.

and conducting adult education programs are producing results sufficient to justify the expenditures. Evaluation also helps determine whether such educational programs are meeting the needs of the adults.

The pursuit of adequate evaluation is important to adult education in two very functional ways. On the one hand, the steadily growing size of the adult education enterprise, which involves millions of people and many more millions of dollars, makes it essential that adult educators be able to defend their programs by knowing its achievements in very specific terms. On the other hand, evaluation provides the field and discipline of adult education with a way of determining the efficiency, effectiveness, and utility of its program planning, its processes, and its management of the instructional situation. Only in this way is it possible to insure that the activity for a particular learning task is suited to the specific group for which it is offered.

Approaches to Evaluation

Adult educators have approached evaluation from the point of view of assessing the program offered and measuring the learning achieved by the participants in a particular instructional activity. In doing this, they have utilized description or fact-finding rather than empirical measurement.

Program evaluation. The marginal character of adult education creates the need for administratively useful measurements of achievement. Administrators are faced constantly with the necessity of justifying their programs to the sponsoring institution in order to continue receiving a measure of available resources. This has prompted the use of a variety of evaluating schemes that can be employed and interpreted in administrative terms. Such schemes are rarely related to or concerned with educational objectives specifically, and they do not measure achievement within the context of a single instructional activity.

The administrative evaluation of programs is accomplished in four principal ways:

1. *By measuring the program against a standard.* This scheme assumes that there is a standard of quality against which any given program can be compared when, in fact, no such standard exists for adult education. The usual procedure, therefore, is to transfer to adult education

the standards set for other, remotely comparable forms or levels of education. Thus, the evening adult school attempts to apply to its program the same standards that are used by the day pre-adult school. The university extension evening program is measured against the standards set for the day program. Standards set by accrediting bodies for regular institutional programs are imposed on adult education without modification and without any recognition of fundamental differences between adult and pre-adult education.

There have been some efforts to create standards for adult education programs. Notable among these is the "clock-hour index," created by Homer Kempfer,[3] which attempts to relate participation in the program to the size of the adult population in the community. There are too many variables in a community which are not taken into account in this formula, so it does not have any real utility as a measure of achievement. This question of standards is one that adult educators tend to shun because of the inherent difficulties encountered in trying to determine standards.

2. *By measuring the program against a hypothetical conception of what a "good" program should be.* There is no general agreement among adult educators as to what constitutes a "good" program. Any conception of "goodness" must fit the particular community in which the program operates, but as yet adult education is too imperfectly developed to establish any criterion for evaluation on this basis.

3. *By measuring against what is done by similar programs in comparable communities.* Since differing local conditions produce different kinds of educational needs and different kinds of available resources, it is not possible to say that a program suited to one community is equally suitable for others. Each community must develop its own particular kind of adult education; therefore, comparisons among communities that are similar in size or other characteristics are odious and meaningless.

4. *By measuring participation.* This is the most common form of administrative evaluation and supports the misconception that success is to be measured by attendance. Participation tends to determine program format and content with the result that many educationally important and socially useful activities that may be unpopular are eliminated. Rural areas with low population density and special needs or interests are penalized by this criterion.

Another form of participation measurement is that concerned with dropouts. This is of equal importance both to administrators and to instructional agents. The dropout rate varies among different adult education activities. Correspondence study, for example, has a consistently higher rate than any other kind of adult education. So little is known

[3] Homer Kempfer, "Formula for Measuring Adult Education Programs," *Adult Education Bulletin* 12 (October, 1948), 195–98. See also his *Adult Education* (New York: McGraw-Hill Book Company, Inc., 1955), pp. 408–11.

about this problem and so many variables are involved that it is virtually useless for program measurement except in the very grossest terms.[4]

Participant evaluation. Systematic adult education has received its greatest impetus within the framework of institutions created to provide education at the pre-adult level. In such cases, the established perceptions of education and of measurement have been transferred to the adult setting; therefore, evaluation is directed toward the measurement of learning accomplished within a specific instructional situation. This usually takes the form of *content measurement* through the use of tests. By all odds this is the most common form of evaluation. It stems from the belief that the principal objective of all education is the acquisition of measurable content and from the fact that content acquired through an educational activity is the easiest item to measure. The standard of achievement in such cases is usually transfered from the ordinary day school program so that an adult is graded in the same way and at the same level of achievement as that used in rating children at a comparable stage of progress in school.

Although content measurement is popular and widely used, it has little intrinsic value in adult education for it has no meaning in terms of the complex of variables that constitute learning. Teacher-made tests are the usual form of content measurement and they have the lowest validity or reliability of any tests. Such tests attempt to measure what the teacher has taught and by no stretch of the imagination do they provide a measure of what an adult may have learned from the educational experience. Standardized achievement tests, such as the General Educational Development Test, have both reliability and validity in terms of the population upon which they were standardized.[5] When the population on which a test was standardized is made up wholly of children and youth rather than adults, and when the test is then used to test adults, the test merely measures an adult's achievement as equivalent to that of children.

The problem of content measurement through testing is beginning to be avoided by adult educators in their search for more meaningful measures of learning achievements. The questionable

---

[4] Edmund deS. Brunner *et al., An Overview of Adult Education Research* (Chicago: Adult Education Association, 1959), pp. 249–53.

[5] Ralph W. Tyler, ed., *The Fact-Finding Study of the Testing Program of the U.S. Armed Forces Institute* (Chicago: The University of Chicago Press, 1954).

utility of tests of this nature tends to discourage the development of standardized measures of achievement suited to adults at various stages in life. More than content measurement is needed to evaluate adult education.

Short-term educational activities, such as meetings or conferences, are often evaluated by using an end-of-meeting reaction slip.[6] This is a very casual attempt to appraise participants' reaction to an educational experience. It has neither validity nor reliability. An attempt to improve the quality of this kind of evaluation has been made through the development of the Kropp-Verner Attitude Scale which measures general attitudes of participants to an adult educational activity.[7]

The Problem of Evaluation

Adequate and meaningful evaluation of adult education involves rigorous social scientific research procedures to develop and test a variety of instruments for measurement that are suited to the infinitely numerous and varied objectives which characterize adult education. Anything less than the most rigorous scientific research is of lesser value. Furthermore, the use of the results of any less reliable research can be misleading and may direct both program planning and management into wrong channels that may counteract any good that might be achieved otherwise. It is better not to evaluate at all than to do so unwisely and ineptly.

This state of affairs is not encouraging to the administrator or to the instructional agent. Obviously, not every adult educator can or will be competent to employ rigorous scientific research procedures when he seeks to evaluate his activities. In time, the discipline of adult education will produce the kinds of evaluation procedures that are needed to measure achievement, and each administrator and instructional agent can contribute to this development by using evaluation wisely and by creating and testing instruments that fall within their range of capabilities.[8]

---

[6] *Effective YMCA Conferencing* (New York: National Board of YMCAs, 1956).

[7] Russel P. Kropp and Coolie Verner, "An Attitude-Scale Technique for Evaluating Meetings," *Adult Education,* Vol. VII (Summer, 1957), 212–15.

[8] For a discussion of samples of evaluations in adult education, see Brunner *et al., op. cit.,* pp. 253–62, and Orville Brim, *Education for Child-Rearing* (New York: Russell Sage Foundation, 1959).

The Evaluation Process

Since evaluation is concerned with measuring changes that result from an educational activity, evaluation at any level and at any degree of precision will follow the same format and progress through the same series of stages. The evaluation process is the same regardless of whether it is a total program in a community or a single instructional session that is being evaluated. The only differences that appear are in terms of the variables to be considered and the scope of the task. Similarly, the same process is applicable to the agent who uses his own somewhat casual instruments and to the social scientist who develops carefully constructed precise instruments for measurement. In this case, differences will appear with respect to the validity and reliability of the instruments and the scientific accuracy and, consequently, the utility of the results.

Before undertaking an evaluation, it is first necessary to answer the question: "Why Evaluate?" Without a clear answer to this question it is not possible to accomplish an effective and useful evaluation of adult education. The purpose of the evaluation will determine the method applied. This purpose may be identified in terms of changes brought about in the learner, the efficiency of the instructional plan and processes, or the impact of the program on the community. An administrator, for example, may evaluate his program in order to determine whether it is meeting the educational needs of all strata in his community. An instructional agent may want to know whether his participants have learned the particular material diffused by the activity. This determination of specific purposes for evaluation affects the nature of the decisions that must be made at each stage in the evaluation process.

The evaluation process consists of four stages which are cumulative and interdependent.[9]

Identification of goals. As discussed elsewhere, the goals of an educational activity identify the purposes for which the activity is conducted and the accomplishments to be expected to result from it. At the time the program is planned, the goals must be identified in specific measurable terms in order that evaluation may be made.

---

[9] Library-Community Project, *Guide to Activities* (Chicago: American Library Association, 1957), p. 16. See also J. Neil Raudabaugh, "Program—Plan of Work—Program Evaluation," *Extension Service Review* (September, 1955).

In most cases, goals and objectives are conceived in broad general terms that are completely useless for purposes of evaluation; therefore, it is necessary to think about evaluation at the time program goals are set. A vague goal, such as "A better appreciation of art," cannot be translated into measurable terms. It does not permit the identification of the specific measurable changes that might be expected to result from the educational experience.

This problem of setting program goals in operational terms is one of the most difficult tasks in adult education. In essence, it involves the identification of specific units in the learning task so that the successful accomplishment of each can be specifically measured. Thus, the setting of operational goals requires a recognition of the particular behavior a program is expected to influence. This behavior may be cognitive, emotional, overt active, or a combination of these. Since behavior can be observed, it can be analyzed and changes in it can be measured.

In setting goals for a program, therefore, the adult educator decides whether he seeks to change attitudes, to develop proficiency in a skill, to establish logical thinking, to enhance perception, to increase knowledge, or any number of similar objectives which can be measured. Not all potential program objectives can be put in measurable terms at present because we have not discovered ways of measuring all things that may result from an educational experience. In every program, however, there are objectives that can be measured.

As with the setting of vague goals, adult educators tend to expect too much achievement from an activity or program. Too many expected results from a single activity can sometimes be just as confusing to evaluate as vagueness. It is better to set simple goals that can be measured than to try to account for all of the variables in a given situation. Enough variables that lie beyond the detection or analysis of the adult educator already exist in society without introducing unnecessary complication and confusion into the controlled instructional setting.

Selection of procedures. With program goals established in operational terms, the next stage in the evaluation process is that of selecting the procedures that will be used to determine the results of the educational process. This involves the construction of a plan for evaluation; therefore, it must be done at the time the program is planned. The planning includes the selection of specific goals to be measured, the choice or construction of instruments to make the necessary measurements, and the development of a schedule of measurement.

The nature of the goals or objectives selected for evaluation tend to predetermine the kinds of instruments and procedures that will be required. A goal involving attitude change obviously requires some kind of attitude measurement before and after the program. Goals related to knowledge or to information in a content area indicate that content testing will be required. As mentioned earlier, not all goals can be measured at present because knowledge and experience in measurement is inadequate. There are some areas of evaluation in which extensive research has been done, while other areas are virtually untouched.[10]

Areas of Measurement

At the moment, there are four major kinds of educational goals that can be evaluated with some confidence. These four areas embrace goals involving knowledge or information, attitude change, skill-learning, and the acceptance or adoption of ideas and practices.

Knowledge or information measurement. Content testing is, perhaps, the oldest form of systematic evaluation. Since testing is used extensively in pre-adult education, the procedures of scientific test construction and standardization are readily available in the literature. In many instances, standardized tests are available in a number of content areas, although since these are often standardized on pre-adult populations they may not be always appropriate for adults.[11] When appropriate tests are not readily available, they can be made by the instructional agent. In such cases care should be exercised to be certain that these instructor-made tests are both valid and reliable. This can be done without too much difficulty by applying standard procedures.

In the construction of tests for adults, unique problems are en-

[10] K. M. Miller, "Evaluation in Adult Education," *International Social Science Bulletin,* Vol. VII, No. 3 (1955).

[11] O. K. Buros, ed., *The Fifth Mental Measurements Yearbook* (Highland Park, N.J.: The Gryphon Press, 1959).

countered. Adults have wide-ranging experience and frequently extensive knowledge related to the material being tested. This must be taken into account. Furthermore, the testing procedure must be perceived by the adult as an integral part of the learning process. Unless the test is meaningful to the adult, both the test and the results will be rejected by him. This action may inhibit or destroy motivation to learn and a low level of achievement may discourage the learner.

Attitude measurement. Attitude modification—with respect both to specific attitude objects and to general attitudes—is frequently identified as a primary or secondary goal of an educational activity. Attitude measurement has received considerable attention from psychologists, social psychologists, and sociologists, so that numerous instruments are available. These, unfortunately, are often difficult to identify since there is no general index to attitude measurement instruments. The procedures for attitude scale construction are well-known and generally available so that an instructional agent can construct an appropriate scale if necessary.[12] Some kinds of attitude scales are relatively simple to construct and to use, while other types are more complex. In some instances the instructional agent should seek assistance and advice from qualified experts to be certain that the instrument devised is suited to the measurement task at hand.

Skill measurement. The performance of learned skills can be measured through observation of performance; however, this procedure is not as simple as it sounds. Accurate observations require a systematic observation schedule to insure that the same operations are observed in the same way each time. To construct such a schedule, it is necessary to analyze the task so that each component element can be isolated and observed independently. If the sequential performance of the elements is a significant part of the learning, this, too, must be accommodated in the schedule. The systematic observation of successive performances provides not only a measure of learning but also an opportunity to vary the rate of learning and to identify the variable difficulty of learning tasks.

Acceptance and adoption measurement. The acceptance of ideas or practices, and their subsequent adoption into the behavior

---

[12] L. L. Thurstone and E. J. Chave, *The Measurement of Attitude* (Chicago: The University of Chicago Press, 1929).

patterns of an individual, constitute an important aspect of adult education. The measurement of adoption is a relatively new concept in the evaluation of adult education. It was introduced by the Cooperative Extension Service. The basic research leading to the development of applicable procedures has been conducted primarily by rural sociologists. Adoption studies have provided not only a measurement of the learning achieved but also an evaluation of the educational process. They have extended knowledge about the characteristics of learners, the adoption process itself, and the role of instruction and communication in achieving acceptance and adoption.[13]

Constructing instruments. In many instances the appropriate instrument for the specific measurement task may not be available. In such cases it is necessary to make an instrument to do the required job. There is adequate knowledge about instrument construction to enable the adult educator to make an instrument that will measure achievement in any of the four goal areas discussed above. Other goal areas will be explored as adult educators approach the task of evaluation from a research point of view.

In constructing instruments, the first task is to identify the situation or response that will provide the necessary evidence of change. This may involve verbal responses to questions or statements, as on a test or scale where the participant answers a question or expresses agreement or disagreement with a statement. It may involve specific behavior or a sequence of specific behavior patterns, such as is involved in the performance of a skill. The form of response must be appropriate to measure the particular learning task.

A second task in the construction of an instrument involves the determination of who will make the measurements. The form of the instrument will be influenced by whether it is to be used by the participant, as in the case of a test, or whether it is to be used by the adult educator, as may be the case with an observation schedule for skill performance evaluation. In either case the same rules apply as are common in the development and construction of instruments for social scientific research.[14]

Every measurement instrument designed for evaluation must have

---

[13] Herbert F. Lionberger, *Adoption of New Ideas and Practices* (Ames, Iowa: Iowa State University Press, 1960). See also Everett M. Rogers, *Diffusion of Innovations* (New York: The Free Press of Glencoe, Inc., 1962).

[14] Mildred Parten, *Surveys, Polls, and Samples* (New York: Harper & Row, Publishers, 1950).

certain qualities that control its effectiveness and which determine the utility of the results.

The instrument must measure what is to be measured clearly and concisely. The instrument must be designed so that it clearly indicates and isolates the particular factors to be measured. There must be no confusion or doubt about what is measured or about what the responses mean with respect to the item being measured. This clarity is the *validity* of the instrument. Validity, in other words, indicates that the instrument always measures what it is intended to measure and nothing more or less.

A standardized test that measures the amount of information on a specific topic that is known by an identified population is a valid instrument for measuring how a specific group compares with that population with respect to the amount of information known about that topic. Thus, if the goal of an evening class is to insure that participants acquire the same amount of information as that acquired in the same class in the day program, then the same test is used for both. If, however, the goal is for participants to learn more about a subject than adults of similar characteristics who have not studied the subject, then a different test is required.

An end-of-meeting reaction slip is an example of an instrument without validity. It does not identify and specify the precise qualities to be measured; therefore, the responses will vary according to the interpretations imposed by the respondent. An attitude scale, on the other hand, is precise in its identification of the factors to be measured so that there can be no confusion among respondents respecting their responses.

The creation of a valid instrument is no simple task and usually requires the assistance of an expert to insure that it will actually measure what it is intended to measure. Measuring instruments are a substitute for direct observation; they have the added advantage of systematizing observation and standardizing the recording of results.

The instrument must supply comparable data consistently from all individuals or situations being measured. When an instrument is so constructed that it permits wide variation in the nature of the measurements recorded from different individuals or different situations, it does not supply usable information. Each instrument should make precisely the same measurements in every situation. This precision is the reliability of the instrument. Again, the reaction slip illustrates the absence of reliability for it seeks individual reactions to a meeting in such a way that different participants interpret the criteria of measurement differently. The scale, on the other hand, measures the same thing in the same way. Without reliability it cannot be known for certain whether differences in response result from differences in the interpretation of the measurement or from differences in the respondent.

The instrument should be simple and economical. Attitudes toward evaluation and measurement can materially influence the response. Simple instruments are less apt to develop negative attitudes than long complicated ones; therefore, they are preferred. Simple instruments also have the advantage of handling separate variables separately so that they can be used to measure different aspects of the learning task at different times. Such a procedure will help to pinpoint areas of achievement or difficulty promptly, so that needed adjustments in the instructional process can be made readily. The urge to achieve simplicity and economy should not lead to a sacrifice of reliability and validity.

Making the Measurements

With the educational goals identified and the appropriate instrument at hand, the next step in the evaluation of adult education involves the use or application of the instrument in order to make the necessary measurements. Since evaluation is concerned with change resulting from an educational experience, and since measurements cannot indicate change unless there is some base line to provide comparison, it is necessary to establish such a base line at the outset. Such a base line should be established prior to or as early as possible in the operation of the program. A base line merely establishes the state of knowledge or proficiency, the attitude, or whatever quality characterizes the objective held by the participant prior to undergoing the educational experience. All subsequent measurements then have a point of reference from which to measure change.

Setting a base line can usually be accomplished by using the same instruments that will be used to measure change. It may be wise to use a different version, form, or battery of the instrument, but a new instrument is not usually needed. The instrument can be altered quite easily by changing the order of questions on a test or reversing a scale. When standardized tests are used, a number of different batteries may be readily available.

In the case of programs which set the acquisition of knowledge or information as a primary goal, a content test can be administered at the start of the program to measure the intensive knowledge about the subject with which participants begin the activity. This test serves the double purpose of setting a base line for measurement as well as advising the agent of the level at which to begin the instruction. Programs concerned principally with attitude change must measure existing attitudes before instruction begins in order to assess change later. The same instrument can usually be used for both measurements.

Periodic measurements during the course of an educational activity provide information relating to the degree and rate of progress of the learner. It is usually wise to employ simple instruments that measure a single specific learning task or component elements of a complex task. This has another function in that it provides the learner an opportunity to know the progress he is making. Awareness of progress is an added incentive to learning. Research indicates that when the learner is made aware of how well he is doing, his rate of learning increases.

Measurement at the end of an activity provides a basis for assessing change when the results of the measurement are compared to those noted in the beginning. In some cases, particularly with respect to acceptance and adoption, measurement must be made at some extended period of time following the conclusion of the activity. Most studies which have utilized both immediate and delayed measurement find differences between the two that may have a significant influence on the planning and management of similar programs.

In the evaluation of programs involving large groups or excessively complex problems, it may be desirable to employ sampling or controlled experiment procedures. In some cases a stratified or random sample of the participants can be tested, rather than the total group. In other cases, the use of control groups may be advisable: a group comparable to the participant group, but which did not undergo the same educational experience, is tested to determine whether changes or differences detected in the participant group can be attributed to the educational experience. This procedure is used frequently in adoption studies, and can be used for pre- and post-testing or for post-testing only.

Utilizing the Results

The use which is made of the results of an evaluation of an adult education program or activity depends in some measure on the purposes for which it was undertaken in the first place. The traditional role of evaluation, particularly in pre-adult education, is that of rating individuals by assigning grades. Although this practice still prevails in certain education situations involving adults, such as credit or diploma courses, it is generally falling into disfavor since grades are meaningless as a measure of learning achievement.

Participants in adult education have their own standards of expected achievement which may or may not coincide with external standards. Evaluation enables the individual to measure his progress toward his own standard. Measurement and comparisons against an external standard or against other learners should not be imposed on an individual in the instructional situation.

Evaluation is most meaningful to the adult educator. It provides the means to assess the effectiveness of instruction, to compare the efficiency of processes, and to analyze the suitability of the content. Thus, he can determine whether the things done in the instructional situation have aided or interfered with the achievement of the goals and objectives.

The use of evaluation should be approached with caution. One frequent error in the use of data supplied through evaluation is that of assuming they show something which they do not actually support. In using the Kropp-Verner Attitude Scale, for example, one cannot assume a scale score reflecting high participant satisfaction with the experience to be a measure of the learning achieved. A participant can enjoy a meeting without learning anything; conversely, he may have learned considerable but be dissatisfied with the way the meeting was conducted.

Adult educators have a responsibility to contribute to the development of the field and discipline by making available the results of their own experience. Carefully controlled studies, or the development and use of new instruments, should be reported to the profession so that others may replicate the study to make further tests of the instrument. Only through the repeated use of the same procedures in different situations and with different groups is it possible to establish fundamental knowledge about the instructional procedures that are most effective for certain learning tasks. Through the continuous evaluation of what we are about in adult education, we can learn how well we are doing and discover ways to do better the tasks society sets for us.

CHAPTER VII

Problems and Prospects

The educational enterprise has not been able to accommodate the rapid expansion of adult education in the past half-century. The opportunities provided by existing educational resources always fall short of the demand for further education and the kinds of learning experiences provided never quite satisfy educational needs. Perhaps no educational system can ever quite meet the demands which society imposes on it, but it can strive for some reasonable adjustment with social need.

Because adult education is marginal and because it has no centrality, the nature and the quality of the adjustment which the field can make to meet society's expectations are somewhat curtailed. There are certain significant barriers to continuing adjustment that are the major problems confronting adult education at present. The solution of these problems will determine its prospects for future development.

Problems

In spite of the many educational opportunities available at present, there still is not enough adult education. Nor is what is available necessarily the right kind. Furthermore, adequate professional leadership is not available. These are fundamental problems that plague the field at the moment.

Coordination. There are many different institutions and agencies offering a wide variety of programs for many different purposes. In spite of this apparent abundance in opportunity, there are many educational needs that are not being met by existing resources. Furthermore, the appropriateness of much of what is available is open to question. The continuing educational needs of certain classes of people seem well provided for, while other kinds of people with different needs have no opportunities available. In general, it appears that the greater the need for education, the fewer the opportunities are available to meet the need.

This imbalance in adult education stems from the absence of any coordinated approach to the problem. Neither coordination nor systematic educational planning has developed extensively on any level. Consequently, there is duplication of effort and a waste of resources on local, state, and national levels. Almost every department of every level of government, for example, is actively engaged in adult education, yet within the governmental structure itself there is not only no coordination of effort but also no awareness of the extent to which government is involved in adult education. Much of what government does in adult education is in direct competition with what other levels or arms of government are doing. Thus, the national government is active in citizenship education for immigrants; the state government promotes fundamental education; and the local government operates elementary education programs for adults. All three levels are providing the same groups with basically the same kind of education, but none has adequate support or draws sufficient participation. By redesigning the structure and content of these three levels, a suitable and adequate education program could be launched with considerable savings in resources. These savings could then be expended in otherwise untouched areas of need. What is true of the governmental structure in this respect is equally true of voluntary and private institutions and agencies.

Patterns of coordination. The need for coordination is self-evident and some attempts to achieve it have been made.[1] The simplest form is that of *informal agreements* among program administrators from several institutions. These agreements tend to set boundaries for spheres of activity, thereby reducing areas of conflict. They may also involve some joint sponsorship of particular programs. Coordination of this sort is minimal, and is usually limited to tacit working agreements respecting educational territory or clientele. It is more apt to be aimed at the preservation of institutional autonomy than at true coordination.

Formal coordination is attempted through existing coordinating instruments, such as general or special councils. In some instances a council for adult education may be created. These councils may involve the professional administrators of the institutions and agencies concerned, or they may include institutional representatives and

[1] W. C. Hallenbeck, *et al., Community and Adult Education* (Chicago: Adult Education Association, 1962), pp. 23–28.

interested citizens. In a study of organization for adult education made in 1954, Olds found special adult education councils existing in some twenty-eight cities.[2] In an attempt to further coordination, The Fund for Adult Education spent considerable money in certain "test" cities, but none of these experiments was notably successful, nor did any survive long after the grant expired. On the whole, the record is abysmal.

Essential factors. There are several factors or conditions that appear to affect the success or failure of coordinating schemes.

Interest. Coordination is not possible unless there is an essential harmony of interests among the instrumentalities being coordinated. Interest in the provision of adequate opportunities for continuing education must be the dominant interest of the institutions being coordinated. Since adult education is almost wholly a marginal activity within the structure of institutions, the necessary level of interest in the institution is not sufficiently high to encourage active coordination. Furthermore, the interest in adult education needs to be directed outward to society rather than inward to the institution so that coordination can dovetail programs with respect to social need and institutional resources rather than concentrate solely on self-interest and institutional aggrandizement.

Function. No coordinating activity can succeed unless there is reasonable agreement among the component units respecting the purposes and objectives of the scheme. Since all institutions involved in adult education are essentially competing for participants and resources, cooperation will not replace competition unless there is agreement that coordination is both necessary and desirable and that all institutions will benefit from it.

Independence. The coordinating instrument must be relatively independent of its constituent bodies in administrative and financial matters. Without such independence, there will be a tendency to assume that the larger institutions dominate the body. Financial support may come from the constituent members on an equitable-share basis, but the coordinating body must not compete with its constituents for support. Adult education institutions and agencies are rarely in a position to provide the necessary support since they themselves are rarely adequately provided for.

---

[2] Edward B. Olds, *Financing Adult Education in America's Public Schools and Community Councils* (Chicago: Adult Education Association, 1954).

Previous experience with adult education councils as a means of coordination has not been encouraging and the prospects for achieving any functional coordination of programs are grim. The need is great and will continue to grow more crucial. Obviously, some new and different system must be created out of a perception of the problem quite different from that which now characterizes thinking in the field. If a solution does not develop, the web of confusion that surrounds adult education at present will continue to grow thicker until eventually it will have to be replaced by a wholly new process for educating adults.

Research. There is a great deal known about educating adults, but not enough. There is a great deal assumed about educating adults on the basis of what is known about education on the preadult level, but these assumptions may not be valid. There is much that needs to be known and access to that knowledge is available, but too few are committed to the advancement of knowledge about adult education. Similar comments can be made about all areas of the social sciences with equal validity. By and large, adult educators are not oriented toward the utilization of research. They share with others doubts about the validity of research on matters that fall within their range of experience. Education and learning are particularly susceptible to such doubt, and adult educators prefer to operate on the basis of experience even though they know that it can and does lead to error. Such fundamental disbelief in the utility of research retards the development of adult education. Through a more extensive use of what is now known, the form, the content, and the quality of the educational experiences operated for adults could be improved immeasurably.

With respect to the production of new research, adult educators are equally indifferent. Although there is a trend toward the increasing use of problem-solving or administrative research, there is too little substantive and fundamental research into the basic unanswered questions about educating adults. Practicing adult educators have little interest, time, or skill to conduct the continuous research necessary to advance the discipline. Foundations are loath to support research on adult education even though they will support basic research in the other social and behavioral sciences. The main incubator for research development is the graduate program in adult education at the several universities but this cannot possibly meet the need of an emerging discipline.

Personnel. The fundamental problem confronting adult education with respect to personnel is the scarcity of people competent to organize and to operate adult education programs. The demand for further education far exceeds the availability of competent administrators or instructional agents. So long as adult education continues as a marginal institutional activity without a well-defined line of career development, this scarcity of personnel is apt to continue. Professionally educated adult educators gravitate toward administrative positions with the result that instructional activities are conducted almost wholly by nonprofessional personnel. The slowly increasing enrollment in graduate programs in adult education and the growth of in-service education promise to alter this situation somewhat.

Prospects

The future prospects for the development of adult education extend beyond the widest horizons of man's imagination. In time it will become such an integral part of human existence that all mankind will be learning systematically all the time. Participation in educational activities will become such a normal part of living for everyone that adult education will cease to have any distinctively identifiable character or form.

But this complete integration of education and life is in the far distance. Its achievement depends upon the direction and acceleration which we give to adult education now. In their *Imperative . . .*, the Professors of Adult Education have identified the conditions that must be met to achieve an educative society: [3]

> 1. There must be a *national perception,* especially on the part of those who control educational policy, of the essential role of continuing education in preventing human obsolescence and in preserving and further developing the American society.
>
> 2. The education of children and youth must be reoriented to a *conception of learning as a lifelong process.* Teachers in schools and colleges must learn to teach youth so that they leave formal schooling

[3] *Adult Education: A New Imperative for Our Times* (Chicago: The Commission of the Professors of Adult Education of the Adult Education Association, 1961), pp. 14–15. See also Webster Cotton, "The Need for Adult Education—Some Major Themes," *Adult Education,* Vol. XIII (Autumn, 1962), 5–12.

(a) with an insatiable curiosity, (b) with a mastery of the tools of learning, and (c) with a commitment to continue learning through the rest of their life span.

3. *The agencies of adult education must clarify their respective tasks* of establishing between themselves orderly working arrangements and interrelated planning and to insure that the resources of adult education are used effectively in meeting the adult educational needs of individuals, institutions, and communities.

4. *A coherent curriculum* of adult education must be developed that provides for the sequential development of the knowledge, understanding, skills, attitudes, and values required to maintain one's effectiveness in a changing social order.

5. The *corps of leaders* and teachers of adults must be enlarged and provided with the knowledge and skills required for them to help adults learn efficiently.

6. A special responsibility is placed on the universities of the country to expand the resources available for *research and advanced professional training* in adult education.

7. Community agencies of adult education, especially schools and colleges, must upgrade the *standards of professional competence* required of those guiding adult learning, and employ personnel with these competencies.

8. There must be a *national commitment* to provide the resources and moral support necessary for the development of lifelong learning as an integral element of the American way of life.

Bibliography

American Educational Research Association, *Review of Educational Research,* Vol. XX, No. 3 (June, 1950); Vol. XXIII, No. 3 (June, 1953); Vol. XXIX, No. 3 (June, 1959).

Batten, T. R., *Communities and Their Development.* London: Oxford University Press, 1957.

Berelson, Bernard, *The Library's Public.* New York: Columbia University Press, 1949.

Bergevin, Paul, and John McKinley, *Design for Adult Education in the Church.* Greenwich, Conn.: The Seabury Press, Inc., 1958.

Bergevin, Paul, Dwight Morris, and Robert M. Smith, *Adult Education Procedures.* Greenwich, Conn.: The Seabury Press, Inc., 1963.

Bode, Carl, *The American Lyceum.* New York: Oxford University Press, 1956.

Brunner, E. de S.,and E. Hsin Pao Yang, *Rural America and the Extension Service.* New York: Teachers College, Columbia University, 1949.

Brunner, E. de S., *et al., An Overview of Adult Education Research.* Chicago: Adult Education Association, 1959.

Cass, Angelica W., *Adult Elementary Education.* New York: Barnes & Noble, Inc., 1956.

Clark, Burton R., *Adult Education in Transition.* Los Angeles: University of California Press, 1956.

Clark, Harold F.,and Harold S. Sloan, *Classrooms in the Factories.* New York: New York University Associate College Press, 1958.

Donahue, Wilma, ed., *Education for Later Maturity.* New York: William Morrow & Co., Inc., 1955.

Ely, M. L., ed., *Adult Education in Action.* New York: American Association for Adult Education, 1936.

Ely, Mary L., ed., *Handbook of Adult Education in the United States.* New York: Bureau of Publications, Teachers College, Columbia University, 1948.

Essert, Paul L., *Creative Leadership of Adult Education.* Englewood Cliffs, N.J.: Prentice-Hall, Inc., 1951.

Grattan, C. Hartley, *In Quest of Knowledge.* New York: Association Press, 1955.

Hallenbeck, Wilbur C., ed., *Psychology of Adults.* Chicago: Adult Education Association, 1963.

Harrison, Harry P., *Culture under Canvas.* New York: Hastings House, Publishers, Inc., 1958.

Hill, Richard, *A Comparative Study of Lecture and Discussion Methods.* White Plains, N.Y.: The Fund for Adult Education, 1960.

Houle, Cyril O., *The Inquiring Mind.* Madison, Wis.: University of Wisconsin Press, 1961.

Houle, Cyril O., *et al.*, *The Armed Forces and Adult Education*. Washington, D.C.: American Council on Education, 1947.

Kelly, Thomas, *A History of Adult Education in Great Britain*. Liverpool: The University Press, 1962.

Kempfer, Homer, *Adult Education*. New York: McGraw-Hill Book Company, Inc., 1955

Kidd, J. R., *How Adults Learn*. New York: Association Press, 1959.

———, *Financing Continuing Education*. New York: Scarecrow Press, Inc., 1962.

Klein, Paul Eugene, *Counseling Techniques in Adult Education*. New York: McGraw-Hill Book Company, Inc., 1946.

Knowles, Malcolm. S., *Informal Adult Education*. New York: Association Press, 1950.

———, ed., *Handbook of Adult Education in the United States*. Chicago: Adult Education Association, 1960.

———, *The Adult Education Movement in the United States*. New York: Holt, Rinehart & Winston, Inc., 1962.

Lindeman, Edward C., *The Meaning of Adult Education*. Montreal: Harvest House, 1961.

Loomis, Charles P., *et al.*, *Rural Social Systems and Adult Education*. East Lansing, Mich.: The Michigan State College Press, 1955.

Lund, Ragner, ed., *Scandinavian Adult Education*. Copenhagen: Danske forlag, 1952.

Lyle, Mary Stewart, *Adult Education for Democracy in Family Life*. Ames, Iowa: The Collegiate Press, 1944.

McMahon, E. E., *The Emerging Evening College*. New York: Teachers College, Columbia University, 1960.

Olds, Edward B., *Financing Adult Education in America's Public Schools and Community Councils*. Chicago: Adult Education Association, 1955.

Peers, Robert, *Adult Education*. New York: Humanities Press, 1958.

Powell, John, *Education for Maturity*. New York: Hermitage House, 1949.

———, *Learning Comes of Age*. New York: Association Press, 1965.

Pressey, Sidney L., and Raymond G. Kuhlen, *Psychological Development Through the Life Span*. New York: Harper & Row, Publishers, 1957.

Rogers, Everett, *Diffusion of Innovations*. New York: The Free Press of Glencoe, Inc., 1962.

Ross, Murray G., and Charles E. Hendry, *New Understandings of Leadership*. New York: Association Press, 1957.

Ross, Leonard Q., *The Education of Hyman Kaplan*. New York: Harcourt, Brace & World, Inc., 1937.

Sheats, Paul H., Clarence D. Jayne, and Ralph B. Spence, *Adult Education: The Community Approach*. New York: Dryden Press, 1953.

Williamson, Maude, and Mary Lyle, *Homemaking Education for Adults*. New York: Appleton-Century-Crofts, Inc., 1949.

Index